Summer Fit Activities™

Second to Third Grade

Build Fit Brains and Fit Bodies!

 Fun, skill based activities in reading, writing, mathematics, and language arts with additional activities in science and geography. Curriculum activities are based on national standards.

 Summer Fitness program includes aerobic and strength exercises.. Fitness log, exercise videos and instructions included. Keeping young bodies active and strong helps children live better, learn more and feel healthier.

 Incentive Contract Calendars motivate children to complete activities and exercises by rewarding their efforts. Summer Explorers are lists of fun and active things to do — perfect for when your child says, "I'm bored, what can I do?"

 Core values and role model activities include child activities, parent talking points and reading lists.

 Summer Journaling, Book Reports, Health and Nutrition Index, Certificate of Completion and Flashcards.

D1314018

Access more summer resource materials at
www.SummerFitActivities.com

Written by: Kelly Terrill and Portia Marin

Fitness and Nutrition: Lisa Roberts RN, BSN, PHN, Coach James Cordova and Charles Miller

Cover Illustration: Amanda Sorensen

Illustrations: Roxanne Ottley, Amanda Sorensen, Fernando Becerra, Richard Casillas, Jason Gould, Bess Li, Sarah Shah

Page Layout: Robyn Pettit

Special Thanks: Wildlife SOS

For orders or product information call 801-466-4272

Dedication

Summer Fit™ is dedicated to Julia Hobbs and Carla Fisher who are the original authors of Summer Bridge Activities™. Julia and Carla helped pioneer summer learning and dedicated their lives to their vocation of teaching.

Caution

Exercises may require adult supervision. If you have any concerns regarding your child's ability to complete any of the suggested fitness activities, consult your family doctor or pediatrician. Children should always stretch and warm up before exercises. Do not push children past comfort level or ability. Exercises were created to be fun for parents and caregivers as well as the child, but not as a professional training or weight loss program. Exercise should stop immediately if you or your child experiences any of the following symptoms: pain, feeling dizzy or faint, nausea, or severe fatigue.

Copyright

ISBN 978-0-9982902-3-2

Table of Contents

Parent Section

Activities and Exercises

Section 1

Section 2

Section 3

Section 4

Section 5

Extras

★ = Academic   ● = Core Value   ▲ = Fitness   ■ = Writing   ◆ = Play & Do   ◆ = Track

Dear Parent,

As a mother, I value giving my children the academic resources they need for success in both their personal and school life. However, when summer comes it is hard to resist the urge to shutter the books and toss the backpacks in the closet.

I have learned first hand that the lack of study over the summer holiday can cause summer learning loss. Studies show that as much as 2.5 months of learning can be undone and some children have lower test scores during the period directly after summer. It is important to find a balance between summer vacation and homework. **Summer Fit Activities** is the resource that does it while looking and feeling like academic summer camp.

Summer Fit Activities is an engaging workbook that helps your child learn and grow. It contains three different foundation pieces for your child's success: academics, health, and values that help children become kinder, more empathetic and stronger leaders. **Summer Fit Activities** makes learning fun with colorful illustrations, family activities, fitness logs, and incentive calendars. Summer Fit is easy to use for parents, caregivers and even grandparents, because day-by-day lesson plans are straightforward and flexible to allow you to create a summer learning experience specifically for your child.

Summer Fit Activities educates the whole child just like you would in summer camp- with an emphasis on FUN. My children love the healthy snack ideas they can make on their own and the Summer Explorer lists of outdoor learning activities that provide hands on learning experiences. I love the flashcards included in the back of book to help reinforce basic skills and the peace of mind knowing that I am teaching my child to be a great person, as well as a great student.

Summer is a time for adventure and fun, but it is also a time of learning and growth. With **Summer Fit Activities** I found the balance I was looking for - unplug, learn and let the magic of summer unfold before your eyes!

Have a wonderful summer,

Christa
Parent

INSIDE
Summer Fit Activities™

Here is what you will find inside Summer Fit™:

Academics

• There are 5 sections of academic exercises, each section with its own core value and journal entry page.

• Sections begin with Incentive Contract Calendars and "Summer Fitness Logs."

• Your child will complete activities in reading, writing, math and language arts. Science and geography activities are included throughout the book.

• When your child completes each day, he/she may color or initial the academic and reading icon for that day on the Incentive Contract Calendar.

• Parents initial the Incentive Contract Calendar once the section has been completed.

Fitness

Research shows that keeping bodies strong and healthy helps children learn better, live better and even miss fewer days of school! To keep bodies healthy, children need to eat right, get enough sleep and exercise daily.

• The Summer Fitness Program helps children set goals and track performance over the summer.

• Daily aerobic and strength exercises

• Fitness & Health Index includes Nutrition page, Foods to Eat Everyday & Meal Tracker.

• Online videos show the proper way to complete exercises.

Values Education

Core values are fundamental to society and are incorporated into our civil laws. Research shows that character education is more effective when parents encourage values in their child's daily routine. Core values are vitally important to the overall growth, well-being and success of all children.

• Each section highlights two different values and role models.

• Value activities are designed for children and parents.

• Each value includes a reading comprehension activity based on role models from throughout the world.

Helpful Hints for Summer Fit™

1 Flip through the book to become familiar with the layout and activities. Look ahead to the upcoming core value so you can incorporate discussions and activities into your daily routine.

2 Provide your child with the tools he/she will need to complete the work: pencils, pens, crayons, ruler, and healthy dose of encouragement.

3 Try to set aside a specific time to do Summer Fit™ each day (for example, after breakfast each morning). Make sure your child has enough time to complete the day's work and exercise.

4 Be a cheerleader! Encourage your child to do their best, urging them to challenge themselves. Make sure they know you are there to help them if they need support. Talk about and reinforce the material in the book beyond the page. For example, after reading about insects, encourage your child to find an insect in the yard to observe and draw.

5 Look at your child's work frequently. Make sure they know you value what they are doing and it is not just "busywork".

6 Try doing Summer Fit™ outside in the fresh air: at the park, in the backyard, camping, or on the beach. Summer Fit™ can go wherever you go!

7 Ask older siblings, grandparents, babysitters and even friends to participate in and give one on one help with the activities. Summer Fit™ is great shared experience!

8 Keep up with the Incentive Contract Calendars. Follow through and reward completed work: stamps, stickers, hugs, and high fives are great ways to motivate and recognize a job well done.

9 Let your child do more than one page at a sitting if he/she is enthusiastic and wants to work ahead. Make sure to check the website for additional activities and resources that can help you tailor Summer Fit™ to your child's needs.

10 When the book has been completed, display the Certificate of Completion proudly and let your child know what a great job he/she did. Celebrate!

Encourage Summer Reading and Writing

Reading and writing skills are important skills for your child's success. Summer is a great time to encourage and build reading and writing skills with your child regardless of ability.

You can do many things to encourage literacy and writing:

 Make Reading a Priority: Create a routine by establishing a reading time each day for your child.

 Read Around Your Child: Read in front of him/her as much as possible. Talk with your child about the books you are reading.

 Create a Summer Reading List: Find books that involve your child's favorite interests like sports, art, mysteries, dance, etc.

 Reading On The Road: Billboards, menus, street signs, window banners and packaging labels are great ways to reinforce reading comprehension skills.

 Storytelling: Have campfire nights in your backyard and tell stories about things you did when you were their age. Slip in a few scary spooks as well!

 Read Together: Newspapers, magazine articles and stories on the Internet are great to read together and discuss.

 Library Time: Go to the library on a weekly basis to choose new books.

 Letter Writing: Encourage your child to write thank you notes and letters.

 Plan a Trip: Have your child plan a trip for the family. Have him/her write an overview of the trip including where, what to bring, how to travel, how long and what you will do on your trip.

 Create a Joke Book: Provide a list of subjects for your child to create jokes about.

Family Writing Hour: Sit down as a family and write a story together. Read the story out loud at the end.

 Script Writing: Ask your child to write a movie script. When it is finished, perform it as a family – be sure to video the production!

 Poetry: Discuss different forms of poetry. Have your child write a poem. Add an illustration.

Mindfulness

As a parent or guardian it is easy to get pulled into the many distractions of daily life. Have you ever wondered if your child has the same difficulties juggling personal interests with school with all the beeps, phone calls and text messages along the way?

Multitasking, compounded with technology, can make it difficult for all of us to concentrate on what we are doing in the moment. Growing research shows that we are hard wired to focus on one thing at a time. Teaching your child to be mindful and to focus on their internal feelings allows your child to fully experience what they are doing in the moment and can have a lasting effect on what, how and why they learn. Learning to sit without distractions and to focus on the moment is a gradual process that has immense benefits for you and your child.

Parent Tips to Help Children Be Mindful

 Time Set a time when all noises, distractions and devices are turned off — start with 5 minutes a day.

 Talk Ask your child to clear her thoughts and to focus on not thinking about anything.

 Focus Focus on breathing, take deep breathes and exhale slowly.

 Quiet Sit in silence.

 Show Show your child gratitude by thanking her for her time. Ask her what she is thankful for and discuss the importance of being grateful.

2-3 • © Summer Fit Activities™

Living Earth Friendly

We all share this home called Earth, and each one of us needs to be responsible in helping take care of her. There are many things families can do together to REDUCE, REUSE, and RECYCLE in order to be kind to Mother Earth. We can all BE SMART AND DO OUR PART!

There are many opportunities each day for us to practice these little steps with our children and we should talk with them about how little things add up to make a big impact.

REDUCE, REUSE, RECYCLE

REDUCE: Means to use less of something. Encourage your children to use water wisely, turn off lights when leaving a room, and use your own bags at the grocery store.

REUSE: Means to use an item again. Refill water bottles, wash dishes and containers instead of using disposable, mend or repair the things you have before buying new, and donate clothes and toys to be used by someone else.

RECYCLE: Means to make a new thing out of an old one. Recycle cans, bottles, and newspapers. Participate in local environmental initiatives like recycling drives.

REBUY: Means to purchase items that have already been used or recycled. Shop at thrift and consignment stores and when possible buy items that have been made from recycled materials.

Summer Fitness Program

Choose a strength or cardio exercise for each day of academic activities. Check the box ✓ each day you complete your fitness activity. Fill in the Fitness Log on the back of each Incentive Contract Calendar. Choose exercises from the Health and Nutrition section in the back of the book. Exercise videos can be viewed at **www.SummerFitActivities.com.**

	Date	Stretch	Activity	Time
1.	*examples:* June 4	Run in place	Sky Reach	7 min
2.	June 5	Toe Touches	Bottle Curls	15 min
3.				
4.				
5.				

Let's Move!

Warm Up! Get ready to exercise by stretching and moving around.

Stretch! Move your head slowly side to side, try to touch each shoulder. Now move your head forward, touch your chin to your chest, then look up and as far back as you can. Try to touch your back with the back of your head.

Touch your toes when standing. Bend over at the waist and touch the end of your toes or the floor. Hold this position for 10 seconds.

Move! Walk or jog in place for 3-5 minutes to warm up before you exercise. Shake your arms and roll your shoulders when you are finished.

Summer Skill Review - Grade 2 READING

Find out where your child needs a little extra practice!

1. Circle the verbs in these sentences.

a. The dog ran across the yard and jumped in the pool.

b. I kicked the ball into the net.

2. Underline the nouns in the following sentences.

a. Jason and Garret washed their father's new car.

b. They sprayed it with the hose then dried it with some fluffy towels.

3. Write the two words that make up the compound word homework.

_____   _____

4. Write a compound word that means a house for a bird.

_____ .

5. Write the correct punctuation   .   ?   !

a. I see a snake _____

b. How old are you _____

c. I am in third grade _____

6. Choose the correct pronoun.

a. One of the girls lost __thAR__ purse.	her	their
b. My brother won __his__ baseball game.	its	his

7. Divide the words into syllables.

a. homework   __home WORK__   2

b. chicken   __2__

c. basketball   __3__

Summer Skill Review - Grade 2 READING

Find out where your child needs a little extra practice!

8. Write the plural for these words.

a. cat _____dog_____   b. fox _____BOX_____   c. baby _____BABY_____

9. Write a synonym for each word.

a. big _____   b. look _____   c. quiet _____

10. Write an antonym for each word.

a. noisy _____   b. shout _____   c. fast _____

11. Write the contraction for each set of words.

a. I will _____   c. he is _____   e. let us _____

b. they will _____   d. we are _____   f. she is _____

12. Write an adjective to describe each word.

a. _____ snake   b. _____ spider   c. _____ feet

13. Write the words in alphabetical order.

bathtub   bucket   brain   below

_____, _____, _____, _____,

14. Choose the correct word.

Yesterday was the _____ day ever!	hot hotter hottest

2

Summer2-3 • © Summer Fit Activities™

SummerSummerFitActivities.com

1. Addition and subtraction

a. 6 + 4 = _____   c. 6 - 4 = _____   e. 7 + 7 = _____

b. 10 + 9 = _____   d. 15 − 5 = _____   f. 8 - 1 = _____

2. Circle the even numbers.

67	14	140	80	16	8

3. Write >,<, =

a. 6 _____ 8   c. 65 _____ 65   e. 3 + 4 _____ 4 + 3

b. 20 _____ 18   d. 21 _____ 12   f. 8 -1 _____ 7 + 1

4. Look for the pattern and write what comes next.

X X O X X O X X 0 _____, _____, _____.

5. Count the tally marks.

    = _____

6. Count by 2's. Fill in the missing numbers.

2, 4, _____, _____, _____, _____, _____, _____, _____, 20

7. Count by 10's. Fill in the missing numbers.

10, 20, _____, _____, _____, _____, _____, _____, _____, 100

8. Circle the digit in the one's place.

22	45	67	99

9. Circle the digit in the ten's place.

36	45	89	76	69

Find out where your child needs a little extra practice!

10. Circle the digit in the 100's place.

345	629	110	490	245

11. Draw a line of symmetry in each shape.

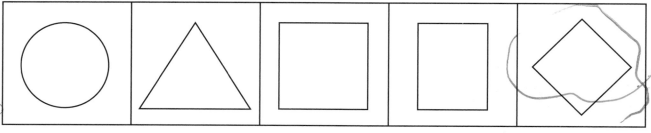

12. Fill in the missing numbers.

a. 16 + 30 + 8 = _____

b. 8 + _____ = 20

c. 10 + 23 = _____ + 10

d. 9 - 2 = 7

13. Write the time shown on the clocks.

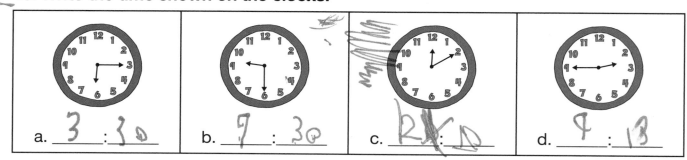

a. 3 : 30

b. 7 : 30

c. _____ : _____

d. 9 : 13

14. There were 10 birds in a tree, 7 flew away. Write a number sentence to how many birds are left in the tree.

_____

15.

a. Draw a hexagon

b. Draw a triangle

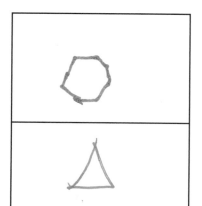

c. Draw a rectangle

d. Draw a square

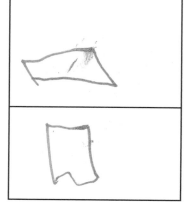

INCENTIVE CONTRACT CALENDAR

My parents and I agree that if I complete this section of

Summer Fit Activities™

and read _____ minutes a day, my reward will be _____

Child Signature: _____   Parent Signature: _____

Day 1	✏️	📖
Day 2	✏️	📖
Day 3	✏️	📖
Day 4	✏️	📖
Day 5	✏️	📖

Day 6	✏️	📖
Day 7	✏️	📖
Day 8	✏️	📖
Day 9	✏️	📖
Day 10	✏️	📖

Color the ✏️ for each day of activities completed.

Color the 📖 for each day of reading completed.

Summer Fitness Log

Choose your exercise activity each day from the Aerobic and Strength Activities in the back of the book. Record the date, stretch, activity and how long you performed your exercise activity below. Fill in how many days you complete your fitness activity on your Incentive Contract Calendars.

	Date	Stretch	Activity	Time
examples:	June 4	Run in place	Sky Reach	7 min
	June 5	Toe Touches	Bottle Curls	15 min
1.				
2.				
3.				
4.				
5.				
6.				
7.				
8.				
9.				
10.				

I promise to do my best for me. I exercise to be healthy and active. I am awesome because I am me.

Child Signature: _____

Synonyms are words that mean almost the same thing. Draw a line to match the synonyms.

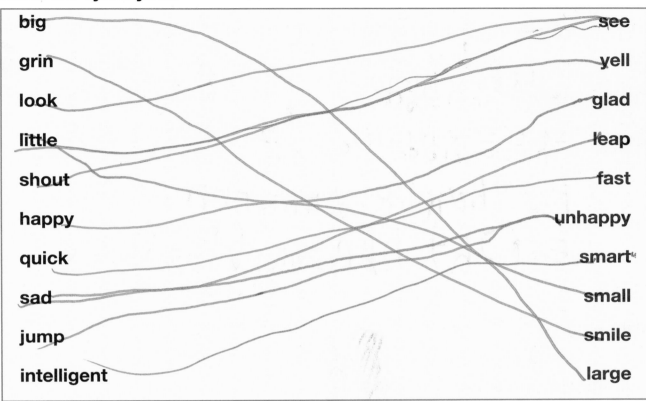

big	see
grin	yell
look	glad
little	leap
shout	fast
happy	unhappy
quick	smart
sad	small
jump	smile
intelligent	large

Circle the synonym for each underlined word.

1. We should be <u>silent</u> in the library.

fast   noisy   (quiet)   silly

2. Mom was happy with the <u>beautiful</u> flowers we gave her.

ugly   (pretty)   yellow   sad

3. It was <u>difficult</u> to ride our bikes up the steep hill.

fast   (hard)   easy   cold

Write each number in words.

1 2 3

415   **four hundred fifteen**

1. 150   _Owe hundred fiftee_

2. 325   _thee hundred 7_

3. 418   _for hundred eateen_

4. 863   _Eight hundred Six e thee_

Write each of these in digits.

Four hundred forty-nine   449

5. Six hundred fifty-two   _652_

6. Three hundred nineteen   _319_

7. Eight hundred seventy-five   _875_

8. One hundred twenty-seven   _127_

Choose your **STRENGTH** exercise!

Day 1

Exercise for today:

PUShUPS

Read the passage about sharks. Answer the questions.

There are more than 300 kinds of sharks. The biggest shark is the whale shark and is longer than a bus! Even though it has more than three thousand teeth, the whale shark is gentle and eats only fish and shrimp. The smallest shark is a dwarf shark and is only as big as the palm of your hand. The great white shark is the most dangerous shark in the ocean. Its teeth are big and sharp and can eat a seal in one bite. A great white shark can be as big as a speedboat.

Sharks are fish. Even though most fish lay eggs, sharks do not. Baby sharks, called pups, are born alive. As soon as the pups are born they are on their own and swim off to hunt for food. A shark has many rows of teeth. When one tooth falls out another one moves up to take its place. Sharks are very good hunters and many will eat almost anything that lives in the ocean, even other sharks.

Circle True if the sentence is True, False if it is not true.

1. Whale sharks are gentle sharks.   True   False

2. Dwarf sharks are huge.   True   False

3. Sharks lay eggs.   True   False

4. Baby sharks are called pups.   True   False

5. Sharks have only a few teeth.   True   False

Write the antonym for each word found in the passage above.

6. more	_____	**biggest**	_____
7. most	_____	**many**	_____
8. good	_____	**anything**	_____

Look at the numbers in each house. Use the numbers to write two correct addition sentences and two correct subtraction sentences.

4, 5, 9   **8, 2, 10**    **5, 8, 13**

1.   **2.**

4 + 5 = 9   8 + 2 = 10   5 + 8 = 13

5 + 4 = 9   2 + 8 = 10   8 + 5 = 13

9 - 4 = 5   2 + 8 = 10 =

9 - 5 = 4

Finish the patterns.

3. **Count by 2s**   2, ____,____,____,____,____,____,____,____, 20

4. **Count by 3s**   3, ____,____,____,____,____,____,____,____, 30

5. **Count by 4s**   4, ____,____,____,____,____,____,____,____, 40

6. **Count by 5s**   5, ____,____,____,____,____,____,____,____, 50

Choose your **AER** BIC **exercise!**

Exercise for today:

Check & Record in Fitness Log.

Day 2

2-3 • © Summer Fit Activities™

SummerFitActivities.com

 **Singular and Plural**

Write the plural version of each word.

1. beach _____

2. fox _____

3. peach _____

4. book _____

5. house _____

6. dog _____

7. boy _____

8. hen _____

9. box _____

10. dress _____

Some words change completely in their plural form.	When a singular word ends in "y" you usually change the "y" to an "i" and add "es."
11. child _____	15. baby _____
12. man _____	16. lady _____
13. woman _____	17. cry _____
14. tooth _____	18. fly _____

Write the numbers in order, beginning with the smallest.

1. 114,   188,   142,   156,   190   _____, _____, _____, _____, _____

2. 295,   246,   287,   305,   223   _____, _____, _____, _____, _____

3. 555,   515,   550,   504,   500   _____, _____, _____, _____, _____

Count the money.

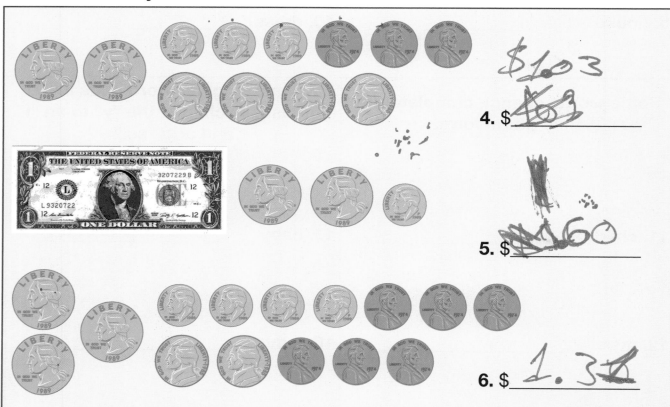

4. $ \$103

5. $ \$160

6. $ 1.3⊄

Choose your STRENGTH exercise!

Exercise for today:

Check & Record in Fitness Log.

12

2-3 • © Summer Fit Activities™

SummerFitActivities.com

Nouns

Nouns are words that name a person, place, or thing. Circle the nouns.

1.	cold	green	shoe	shark
2.	fast	sun	hot	owl
3.	zoo	sick	smile	rocket
4.	stinky	ant	corn	house

5. Think of a noun to fill in each blank.

The ____BIKe____ barked at the ____PaRK____.

I rode my ____BIKe____ to the ____PaRK____.

The baby sat on the ____ChAR____ and laughed.

I used my birthday money to buy a ____BARR____.

Circle the nouns in the sentences below.

6. We built a campfire and roasted marshmallows.

7. The children ran across the bridge and jumped into the water.

8. The bird flew to the highest branch of the tree.

9. My sister and I went to the zoo and saw many animals.

1. Which holds less?	2. Which is longer?
pints cups	feet inches

3. Draw hands on the clock to show 3:45.

4. What time was it 2 hours ago?

_____ : _____

5. Write the time in two ways.

_____ : _____ Quarter past _____

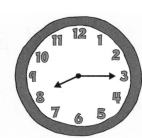

6. Circle the month that comes after June.

August	July

Circle the month that comes before December.

March	November

Choose your AEROBIC exercise!

Day 4

Exercise for today:
_____

Check & Record in Fitness Log.

HONESTY

Honesty means being fair, truthful, and trustworthy. People who are honest do not lie, cheat or steal. Honesty is telling the truth no matter what.

Honest Abe. Abraham Lincoln was the 16th president of the United States and was known for his honesty. Even before he became president, Abe Lincoln was known as a person who was honest and truthful. When he was a young storekeeper, Mr. Lincoln discovered that a customer had overpaid for her groceries. That night after closing up his shop, he walked three miles to the woman's house to pay back the money she had overpaid. Abe Lincoln was truthful and sincere and his honesty made people trust him.

Antonyms are words that have the opposite meaning of each other. Draw a line from each word to its antonym.

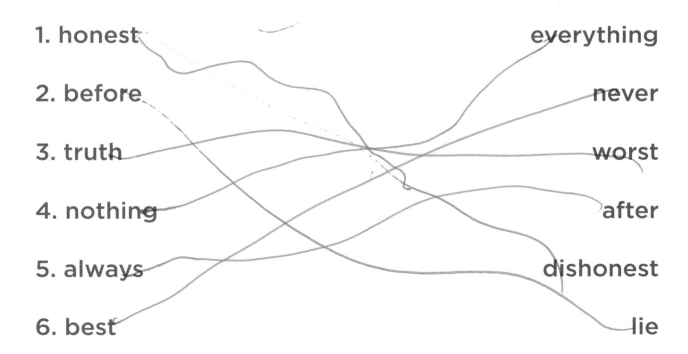

1. honest   everything

2. before   never

3. truth   worst

4. nothing   after

5. always   dishonest

6. best   lie

Value:

HONESTY

Being honest means to be truthful in what you say and do. It means that you do not lie, cheat or steal. Sometimes this can be difficult, especially when we are scared or ashamed about something we did. Sometimes it takes courage to be honest, especially when it is uncomfortable.

"Whatever you are,
be a good one"
-Abe Lincoln

What does honesty look like? Choose an honest action below and draw a picture to represent it in the picture frame.

- I cheat on a test.
- I keep a promise.
- I play fair.
- I take a candy bar from the store without paying.
- I take money out of my dad's wallet without asking.
- I find $5.00 at the library and take it to the front desk.

HONESTY PLEDGE

I promise to tell the truth every day. I will be honest in what I do and what I say.

My Signature

How does it feel when someone lies to you?

SAd

Summer Explorer
Discover New Things to Play and Do!

- Visit the library and get a card if you do not have one.

- Make a fort out of blankets and sheets.

- Make a biodegradable bird feeder and hang it in the yard.

- Have a lemonade stand get your friends to help.

- Play flashlight tag.

- Visit a fire station. Does your family have a plan of what to do in case of fire? Plan a family fire drill.

- Sign up for a free summer reading program at your local bookstore.

- Go for a walk.

- Look up and find figures in the clouds.

- Play an outdoor game like "Simon Says" or "Kick the Can" with family or friends.

- Go for a bike ride.

- Pick up trash around your neighborhood and recycle.

- Find an ant colony. Drop some crumbs and observe what happens. Stay away from fire ants.

- Build a castle or fort out of Legos or blocks.

- Use a recycled plastic bag to create a parachute that will slowly fall to the ground.

- Watch a sunrise or sunset, paint a picture of it.

- Run through the sprinklers.

- Make S'mores and tell ghost stories under the stars.

- Create an obstacle course. Invite your friends and time them to see how fast they complete it.

Biodegradable Birdfeeder

  1 Collect your supplies: peanut butter, birdseed, oranges, and string for hanging.

2 Tie a long string around the pinecone or toilet roll before spreading peanut butter on them and rolling in birdseed. Cut an orange in half, scoop out fruit and fill with birdseed. Attach strings to hang feeder in branch.

 3 Hang your bird treat in the yard and watch for your feathered friends to come and feast.

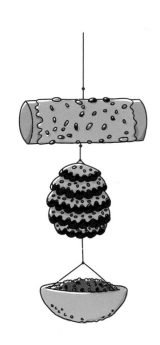

Summer Journal 1

Write about your favorite outdoor summer activity.

Example: Camping, swimming or biking

swimping is the best I Love it
me and my sisty going to.

An abbreviation is usually a shorter form of a word. Abbreviations begin with capital letters and end with periods. Write the abbreviation for each underlined word.

Example: My birthday is <u>January</u> 14th.   Jan.

1. Our neighbor, <u>Mister</u> Smith, is in the hospital.   _US_

2. The baseball game is <u>Saturday</u> at 3 o'clock.   _SAT_

3. <u>Doctor</u> Laks gave me a check-up.   _DOC_

4. I am going to the pool on Seashore <u>Avenue</u>.   _AVC_

5. We picked five <u>pounds</u> of apples at my uncle's orchard.   _POll_

6. There are 31 days in the month of <u>October.</u>   _OCt_

7. Write the abbreviation for each day of the week.

Sunday	Monday	Tuesday	Wednesday	Thursday	Friday	Saturday
Ex. Sun.	mon	tUe	wd	thu	Fr	SAt

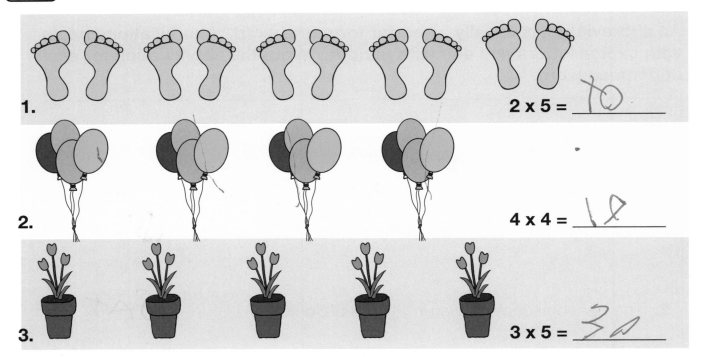

1. 2 x 5 = __10__

2. 4 x 4 = __12__

3. 3 x 5 = __30__

4. Farmer Jon had 6 chickens. Each laid 2 eggs. How many eggs did Farmer Jon have?

6 x 2 = __8__

5. Multiply to solve.

2 x 1 = __3__   2 x 3 = __5__   2 x 4 = __6__   2 x 5 = __7__   2 x 6 = __8__

2 x 7 = __9__   2 x 8 = __10__   2 x 9 = __11__   2 x 10 = __12__   2 x 11 = __13__

Choose your AEROBIC exercise!

Day 6

Exercise for today:

Check & Record in Fitness Log.

Frogs are amphibians. They lay their eggs in water. The baby frogs hatch from jellylike eggs and are called tadpoles. Tadpoles live in the water until it becomes a frog. First, the tadpole grows its back legs, and then it grows its front legs. The tail gets shorter as the legs grow. When the lungs develop the tadpole's transformation is complete. Now a frog, the tadpole hops out of the water and onto land. Frogs like wet places. They have webbed feet and can swim fast. The frog's long sticky tongue makes it easy to catch insects.

Label and color the lifecycle of a frog.

PInK   PInK   PInK

Fill in the blanks.

1. Frogs are _JUmpy_____.

2. Baby frogs hatch from eggs and are called _Kids_____.

3. Frogs like wet _Feete_____.

4. Their _EBs_____ feet help them swim fast.

5. Frogs like to eat _____.

Write the answer on the line.

1. Noah has 6 dimes, how many more dimes does he need to make a dollar? _____

2. If he has 4 dimes, how many more dimes does he need to make a dollar? _____

3. How many quarters are in a dollar? _____

4. How many nickels make .50 cents? _____

5. You have $2.00 and spend .80 cents. How much do you have left? _____

6. Dave had $1.00 and wants to buy a yo-yo for $2.00. How much more money does he need? _____

Choose your STRENGTH exercise!

Day 7

Exercise for today:

_____

Check & Record in Fitness Log.

What is the Category?

Circle the words that answer the question.

1. Which ones are kinds of flowers?

daisy   rose   pine   sunflower   tulip

2. Which animals live in the ocean?

shark   beaver   sting ray   dolphin   swordfish

3. Which would you find at the zoo?

elephant   zebra   monkey   clown   lion

4. Which can you wear?

shoes   stove   hat   coat   socks

5. Which ones are states?

Arizona   China   Utah   Michigan   Alaska

Name three instruments: _____, _____, _____.

Name three fruits: _____, _____, _____.

Name three birds: _____, _____, _____.

1. Write the number that comes before and after.

_____ 125 _____   _____ 89 _____

_____ 111 _____   _____ 345 _____

_____ 200 _____   _____ 67 _____

2. Circle the units you could use to measure length.

centimeters   gallons   inches   feet   ounces

Circle the units you could use to measure liquid.

gallon   feet   quart   ounce   pound

3. Multiply by 3s.

3 x 1 = _____   3 x 2 = _____   3 x 3 = _____   3 x 4 = _____   3 x 5 = _____

3 x 6 = _____   3 x 7 = _____   3 x 8 = _____   3 x 9 = _____   3 x 10 = _____

Choose your AEROBIC exercise!

Exercise for today:

_____

Check & Record in Fitness Log.

Day 8

2-3 • © Summer Fit Activities™

Homophones

A homophone is a word that is pronounced the same as another word, but has a different meaning.

Use the correct homophone to complete each sentence.

four	know	sun	see	pair	bare
for	no	son	sea	pear	bear

1. The _____ came out of his cave and growled.

2. The walls looked _____ when we took down the posters.

3. I _____ my multiplication facts.

4. When I asked for a cookie, my mother said, "_____."

5. I picked a juicy _____ from the tree.

6. My grandma sent me a new _____ of shoes.

7. The summer _____ felt hot on my face.

8. The man and his _____ went fishing together.

9. The great white shark is the fiercest shark in the _____.

10. Can you _____ without your glasses?

11. My brother had a party at the zoo _____ his birthday. He was

turning _____ years old.

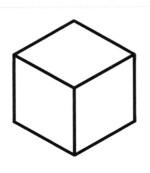 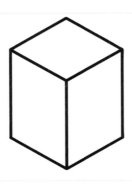 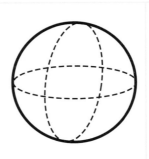 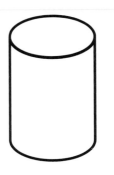

Color the cube blue.   Color the cylinder red.

Color the sphere yellow.   Color the rectangular prism green.

Draw a line of symmetry through each shape.

Ex:

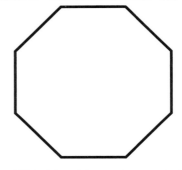

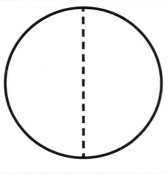

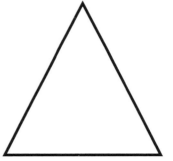

 Choose your STRENGTH exercise!

Exercise for today:

 **Day 9**

2-3 • © Summer Fit Activities™

Compassion is caring about the feelings and needs of others.

A Mother to All

Mother Teresa was a tiny nun with a big heart. As a young woman she decided she wanted to be a missionary in order to spread love and compassion in the world. Mother Teresa spent her life taking care of all the people who had nobody to take care of them: the poor, orphaned, sick, dying, and alone. She had the courage and compassion to care for thousands of people who were unwanted and unloved and she did it without asking for anything in return.

Circle the acts that show compassion, cross out the ones that do not.

I help those in need.

I do not share with others.

I think about how my actions affect others.

I say mean things.

I apologize when I hurt someone.

Value:

COMPASSION

Having compassion means showing kindness, caring and a willingness to help others who may be sick, hurt, poor, or in need. When you have compassion you are putting yourself in someone else's shoes and really feeling for them. You can do this in very small ways for example when your friend trips and falls. You can do this in larger ways when someone you know does not have enough food to eat.

> "Love and compassion are necessities not luxuries. Without them, humanity cannot survive."
>
> – Dalai Lama

Unscramble the letters to reveal the traits of being a Hero of Compassion.

dnik

ufltuhgtoh

aricgn

udantnesinrgd

epilngh

ielgnsnti

rstceandoei

ronfmoicgt

avber

tpaenti

Make a "Compassion Jar". Cut out several slips of paper and write on each a way to show compassion. For example: Hold the door for someone, smile at a stranger, or read to a younger child. Choose one to do each day.

(kind) (thoughtful) (caring) (understanding) (helping)

(listening) (considerate) (comforting) (brave) (patient)

Day 10 — Choose a Play or Exercise Activity!

INCENTIVE CONTRACT CALENDAR

My parents and I agree that if I complete this section of

Summer Fit Activities™

and read _____ minutes a day, my reward will be _____

Child Signature: _____   Parent Signature: _____

Day 1			Day 6		
Day 2			Day 7		
Day 3			Day 8		
Day 4			Day 9		
Day 5			Day 10		

 Color the for each day of activities completed.

 Color the for each day of reading completed.

Summer Fitness Log

Choose your exercise activity each day from the Aerobic and Strength Activities in the back of the book. Record the date, stretch, activity and how long you performed your exercise activity below. Fill in how many days you complete your fitness activity on your Incentive Contract Calendars.

	Date	Stretch	Activity	Time
examples:	June 4	Run in place	Sky Reach	7 min
	June 5	Toe Touches	Bottle Curls	15 min
1.				
2.				
3.				
4.				
5.				
6.				
7.				
8.				
9.				
10.				

I promise to do my best for me. I exercise to be healthy and active. I am awesome because I am me.

Child Signature: _____

SummerFitActivities.com

Reading Comprehension

Read the story and answer the questions below.

Skateboarding is a great sport and can be a fun form of exercise. A skateboard is a fiberglass or wood board mounted on four wheels. A skateboard has four parts: the deck, griptape, trucks and wheels. The deck is the board where you put your feet. On the deck are sandpaper strips that help your feet keep their grip. The trucks are the metal parts that connect the wheels and allow for turns. The wheels, of course, get you where you want to go.

People skate for many reasons. Some skate for fun, some like to do tricks, and some like to compete. An "Ollie" is a basic skateboarding trick where the skateboarder pops the skateboard into the air. Skateboarding can be dangerous so it is important to always wear a helmet.

Circle all the plural words in the story above, then circle the correct answers to the questions below.

1. A skateboard has_____.   6 parts   4 parts

2. The griptape keeps your feet from _____.   slipping   jumping

3. You should always wear a _____ when skateboarding.   helmet   watch

4. Skateboarding is a great form of _____.   exercise   homework

1. Write the signs for less than (<) greater than (>) or equal to (=).

40 _____ 35   23 _____ 32   167 _____ 187

200 _____ 300   144 _____ 144   635 _____ 535

2. Solve the problems by adding or subtracting. Then, fill in the correct sign: (<), (>), or (=).

Ex: 10 + 5 = 12 + 3   8 - 8 ____ 10 - 8   10 + 10 ____ 30 - 10

7 + 7 ____ 6 + 8   20 – 4 ____ 18 + 5   12 – 2 ____ 15 – 4

200 + 50 _____ 100 + 100   400 - 200 _____ 300 - 100

3. Continue the Patterns.

A B B A B B _____, _____, _____, _____, _____, _____.

4. Continue the patterns.

   _____, _____, _____, _____, _____

 _____, _____, _____, _____, _____

 Choose your **STRENGTH** exercise!

 **Day 1**

Exercise for today:

_____

32

2–3 • © Summer Fit Activities™

SummerFitActivities.com

A contraction is the shortening of a word by removing letters and replacing with an apostrophe.

Use these contractions in the blue boxes to replace the words on the right.

he'll	**can't**
it's	**won't**
they're	**we're**
wasn't	**didn't**
she's	**they've**
he's	**we'll**

1. he is _____

2. did not _____

3. will not _____

4. they have _____

5. was not _____

6. she is _____

7. can not _____

8. he will _____

9. we are _____

10. we will _____

11. it is _____

12. they are _____

Draw a line to match the words with the correct contraction.

I'll   does not

shouldn't   has not

doesn't   I will

you're   that is

hasn't   should not

that's   you are

Ex: 4 + __6__ = 10

1. Find the missing number to complete the addition and subtraction facts.

3 + ____ = 10	12 - ____ = 6	8 + ____ = 16	18 - ____ = 9
9 - ____ = 4	____ + 7 = 14	14 + ____ = 20	100 - ____ = 40
4 + ____ = 13	____ - 3 = 15	100 + ____ = 500	50 + ____ = 100

2. Count by 5's. Fill in the missing numbers.

5, _____, 15, _____, 25, _____, 35, _____, 45, _____,

55, _____, 65, _____, 75, _____, 85, _____, 95, _____

3. Maya got $1.00 for her allowance. She spent .26 cents on a cookie.
Cross out the coins to show how much she has left.

_____

Day 2

Choose your AEROBIC exercise!

Exercise for today:

_____

Check & Record in Fitness Log.

Compound Words

Match a green banana to a yellow banana to make compound words. Write the new word on the line.

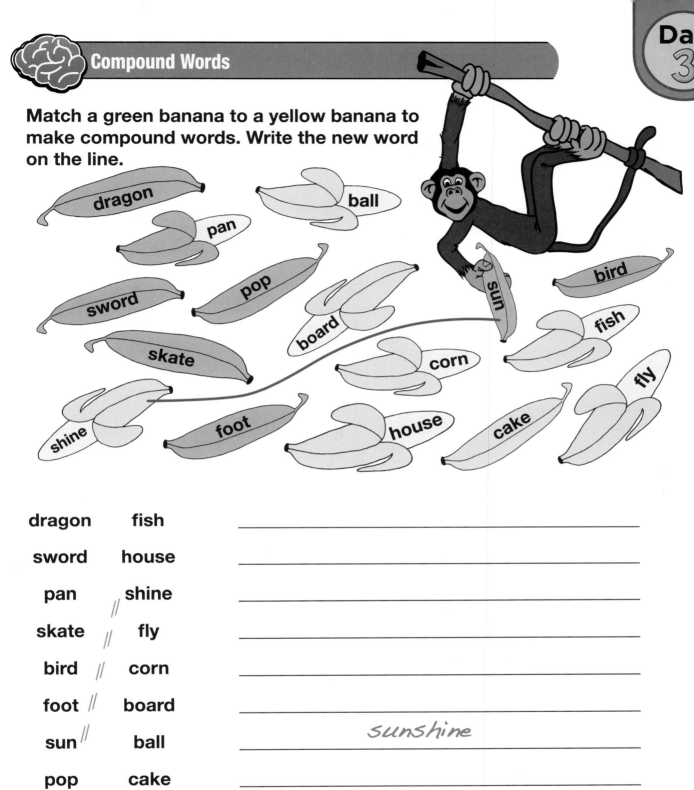

dragon	fish
sword	house
pan	shine
skate	fly
bird	corn
foot	board
sun	ball
pop	cake

_____

_____

_____

_____

_____

sunshine

_____

Think of 4 more compound words. Write them on the lines.

1. _____   2. _____

3. _____   4. _____

Expanded Form

Write each number in expanded form.

Ex.   428 = <u>400</u> + <u>20</u> + <u>8</u>

1. 563 _____ + _____ + _____	4. 875 _____ + _____ + _____
2. 916 _____ + _____ + _____	5. 1,624 _____ + _____ + _____ + _____
3. 4,383 _____ + _____ + _____ + _____	6. 6,957 _____ + _____ + _____ + _____

Write the numbers.

7. 200 + 60 + 4 = _____

8. 100 + 80 + 9 = _____

9. 500 + 10 + 3 = _____

10. 1,000 + 600 + 40 + 8 = _____

11. 3,000 + 200 + 60 + 3 = _____

12. 9,000 + 400 + 20 = _____

Choose your STRENGTH exercise!

Exercise for today:

_____

Day 3

Check & Record in Fitness Log.

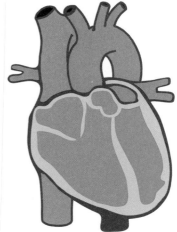

Put your fingers in your ears, close your eyes, and listen carefully. The lub, dub, lub, dub, you hear is the sound of your heart beating. Your heart is a muscle that is located in your chest and is protected by your rib cage. The heart is made up of four chambers, the left atrium, the right atrium, the left ventricle, and the right ventricle. Your heart is about the size of your closed fist and moves blood in and out by expanding and contracting.

Your heart pumps blood through your body every second of your life. You can feel this powerful pumping when you hold two fingertips to your wrist on the thumb side. This is called the pulse. Your pulse rate is the number of beats your heart makes in one minute. When you are at rest, your pulse rate is lower than after you exercise. To find your own pulse, count how many beats per minute when you are still. Count for another minute after you have done some exercise. Can you feel the difference?

Fascinating Facts

1. Your heart beats with enough strength to shoot a stream of blood 30 feet away.

2. The human heart is almost entirely muscle and has the strength to lift about 3,000 lbs.

3. The heart pumps about a million barrels of blood every day.

Choose a word to fill in each blank.

| rib cage | faster | four | pulse | fist | blood |

Your heart is as big as your _____, and is protected by

your _____. The heart pumps _____

throughout your body and is made up of _____ chambers.

The _____ measures how many beats your heart beats

per minute. Your pulse rate is _____ after exercise.

Perimeter is the distance around a shape.

Add the lengths of each side to find the perimeter.

1.

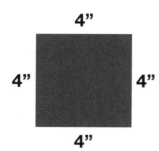

4"

4"   4"

4"

= _____ inches

2.

6"

4"   4"

6"

= _____ inches

3.

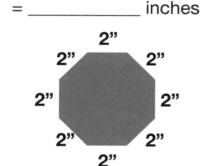

2"

2"   2"

2"   2"

2"   2"

2"

= _____ inches

4.

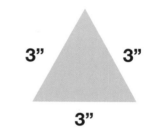

3"   3"

3"

= _____ inches

5. The perimeter around Sam's yard is 30 feet. Look at the diagram. What is the length of the 4th side?

_____

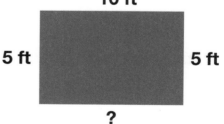

10 ft

5 ft   5 ft

?

Choose your AEROBIC exercise!

Exercise for today:

Check & Record in Fitness Log.

Day 4

Value

Trustworthiness is being worthy of trust. It means people can count on you, and you keep your word.

Harriet Tubman was a slave before the Civil War. Being a slave meant that she had no property, no rights, and had to do whatever her master told her. From a very young age, Harriet had to work hard and even as a little girl, she dreamed of freedom. Although she was small, Harriet grew to be strong and was even more strong-willed. When she was an adult, Harriet escaped and became free, and wanted to help others be free also. She led hundreds of slaves to freedom through the "Underground Railroad, " which was a secret system of hiding places and people that helped the slaves escape. Her nickname was "Moses" after Moses in the Bible. At one time there was a $40,000 reward offered by the slave owners for her capture. Each time she went back to help more slaves, she risked her life. Harriet Tubman is a hero of trustworthiness because people trusted her with their lives and she never let them down.

Read each statement, write T if it is True, and F if it is False.

1. Harriet Tubman had no rights as a slave. _____

2. She was always treated well as a slave. _____

3. Harriet escaped and became free. _____

4. She helped hundreds of other slaves to freedom. _____

Value: TRUSTWORTHINESS

FAMILY ACTIVITIES

Choose one or more activities to do with your family or friends.

Let's talk about it...

Talk with your child about keeping a promise. Help them to understand that it is important to think before they promise something. Be consistent when you are making promises to your children either in rewards or punishments. Lead by example and make sure to follow through with what you say.

 Talk about ways you show you are trustworthy. Remember that when you are dishonest and not truthful, people will not trust you. Think about the times you have been trustworthy. Write down at least 5 words that describe how you felt being trusted.

 Talk about what it means to be a trustworthy friend. Make a Friendship bracelet and give it to one of your friends. Let them know they can count on you to be a good friend.

 Write down the word TRUSTWORTHY. How many little words can you make from the letters?

VALUES ARE A FAMILY AFFAIR

Read more about TRUSTWORTHINESS

Harriet Tubman
By Kathleen Kudlinski

Shiloh
By Phyllis Reynolds Naylor

The Trial of Anna Cottman
By Vivian Alcock

Choose a game or activity to play for 60 minutes as a family or with friends today!

Day 5
Choose a **Play** or **Exercise** Activity!

2-3 • © Summer Fit Activities™

Summer Explorer
Discover New Things to Play and Do!

- Play in the rain. Make mud pies and jump in puddles.

- Have a book exchange with your friends.

- Finger paint.

- Make your own musical instruments out of cardboard boxes and perform a song.

- Create a healthy dinner menu for your family.

- Visit a lake, river, or pond. Bring a notebook to do some nature drawings.

- Make your own bubble solution. Go outside and make some enormous bubbles.

- Pick wildflowers and arrange them in a glass or jar.

- Draw a flipbook.

- Make cookies for a neighbor — deliver them with a parent.

- Go to the park with a friend.

- Sign up for a free project at Home Depot, Lowes, or Michaels.

- Make a scavenger hunt to do with friends or family.

- Plant something: flowers, vegetables, herbs, a tree.

- Read to a younger sibling.

- Make a photo album or scrapbook.

- Try a new cookie recipe.

- Have a water balloon fight.

- Help an elderly neighbor weed his/her garden.

- Paint or draw a self-portrait.

Giant Bubbles

6 cups Water
1/2 cup Dish Soap (Dawn blue)
1/2 cup Cornstarch
1 TBSP Baking Powder
1 TBSP Glycerin
(Glycerin found in cake decoration aisle at craft store)

 Slowly mix together in large bucket or dishpan.

 Let solution sit for 1-2 hours.

 Tie a length of string between two straws to make a bubble wand or use store bought wands. The bigger your wand, the bigger your bubbles!

Summer Journal II

Write about your family vacation.

2-3 • © Summer Fit Activities™

Adjectives are words used to describe another person or thing in a sentence. Think of an adjective, or two, to describe each noun. Draw a picture to illustrate your phrase.

Ex: Creepy, old house

1. _____ feet

2. _____ worm

3. _____ tree

4. _____ ice cream

5. _____ spider

6. _____ elephant

Circle the adjectives in each sentence.

7. My older brother has a shiny, new, red car.

8. I like to go swimming in the cool, blue lake on hot, summer days.

2-3 • © Summer Fit Activities™

1. Round the numbers to the nearest 10.

54 _____   86 _____   45 _____

29 _____   41 _____   13 _____

78 _____   61 _____   89 _____

2. Round to each 10 to estimate the sums.

46 + 21 = _____   59 + 11 = _____

22 + 19 = _____   68 + 12 = _____

3. Write the number.

10 more than 43 = _____   10 less than 90 = _____

10 more than 76 = _____   10 less than 75 = _____

100 more than 615 = _____   100 less than 344 = _____

100 more than 180 = _____   100 less than 650 = _____

Choose your AEROBIC exercise!

Exercise for today:

Day 6

Check & Record in Fitness Log.

Analogies

Choose a word to fit the analogy.

Ex: Read is to book as write is to letter.

1. Cat is to kitten as dog is to _____.

2. Up is to down as in is to _____.

3. Eye is to see as ear is to _____.

4. Fish is to swim as bird is to _____.

5. Apple is to fruit as corn is to _____.

6. Girl is to woman as boy is to _____.

Add to find the sums.

1.	2.	3.
8	7	10
6	2	12
+ 5	+ 6	+ 16
———	———	———

4.	5.	6.
22	13	34
14	20	21
+ 10	+ 16	+ 42
———	———	———

Place value.

Ex: 56 = 5 tens 6 ones

7. 48 = _____ tens _____ ones   8. 63 = _____ tens _____ ones

9. 98 = _____ tens _____ ones   10. 75 = _____ tens _____ ones

Ex: 2 tens + 5 ones = 25

11. 7 tens + 6 ones = _____   12. 8 tens + 9 ones = _____

13. 1 ten + 8 ones = _____   14. 3 tens + 3 ones = _____

Choose your STRENGTH exercise!

Exercise for today:

Check & Record in Fitness Log.

Day 7

Fill in the vowel pairs to complete each word.

oa	ee	ai	ea	oo

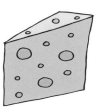

p _____ l   f _____ t   b _____ t   p _____ ch

p _____ nt   g _____ t   s _____ p   b _____ t

ch _____ se   h _____ p   sh _____ p   r _____ n

Tally Chart

Look at the tally chart and answer each question.

Favorite Sports

basketball	soccer	football	tennis	volleyball
IIII III	IIII IIII	IIII IIII	IIII I	IIII I

1. Which sport is the favorite? _____

2. Did more people choose basketball or football? _____

3. How many more people chose soccer than tennis? _____

4. What 2 sports were both chosen by 6 people? _____

Show the time on each digital watch.

quarter after 5

Ex: `5:15`

5. half past 3

6. twenty after one

7. five to nine

8. ten after eleven

9. quarter to one

Choose your AEROBIC exercise!

Exercise for today:

Check & Record in Fitness Log.

Day 8

Perfect Punctuation

Match each punctuation mark with the correct name.

.	comma
?	exclamation point
,	question mark
!	period

Use the correct punctuation marks for each sentence.

1. Do you like camping _____

2. My favorite part of camping is sleeping under the stars _____

3. We like to eat hot dogs, hamburgers, and chips _____

4. Watch out _____ The fire is hot _____

5. Have you ever made s'mores _____

6. Camping is a great summer activity _____

7. Asking sentences begin with a capital and end with a question mark.
They often begin with these words: how, did, can, is, should, and would.
Write three asking sentences about camping.

How _____

Can _____

Did _____

8. Telling sentences begin with a capital and end with a period.
Write a telling sentence about camping.

_____

_____

_____

1. Circle the name of this shape:

pentagon   square

It has _____ sides and _____ vertices.

2. Circle the name of this shape:

octagon   triangle

It has _____ sides and _____ vertices.

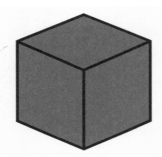

3. Can you stack this shape?

yes   no

Can you roll this shape?

yes   no

4. Draw 2 lines of symmetry through this shape.

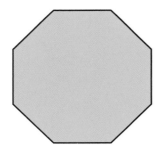

5. Finish the shape by drawing the symmetrical half.

 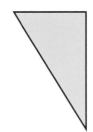

Choose your STRENGTH exercise!

Exercise for today:

_____

Day 9

Check & Record in Fitness Log.

2-3 • © Summer Fit Activities™

SELF-DISCIPLINE

Self-discipline is to have control of your actions to enable you to achieve your goals. Self-discipline includes self-control and dedication.

Value

Stephanie Lopez Cox works hard to reach her goals. Her focus and dedication helped her gain a spot on the U.S. National Women's Soccer Team that won a gold medal at the 2008 Beijing Olympics. Stephanie practices very hard and is committed to doing what it takes to make her the best athlete, soccer player, and person she can be. In college and high school she was known for her excellent soccer skills as well as her diligence to her schoolwork. Stephanie recognizes the importance of displaying self-discipline in all that she does. She is also dedicated to charity work and focuses on helping children who live in foster care.

List three things that help Stephanie reach her goals:

1. _____

2. _____

3. _____

Think of a goal you would like to reach. Now, write down things you can do to accomplish that goal.

1. _____

2. _____

3. _____

Value: SELF-DISCIPLINE

FAMILY ACTIVITIES

Choose one or more activities to do with your family or friends.

 Plan to exercise together as a family this week. Have a family walk after dinner. Choose an activity to do together. Hike, bike, swim, dance and play together. At night, play a game of "flashlight tag." Whoever gets "tagged" by the light is "it."

 Give up TV for a day, a week, or longer. Instead, spend time outside, reading, or with family and friends.

 Plan a sequence of events or activities to do in one day. Before you move on to the next one you must finish the one before it.

VALUES ARE A FAMILY AFFAIR

Read more about SELF-DISCIPLINE

The Chocolate Touch
By Patrick Catling

The Great Kapok Tree
By Lynne Cherry

Miss Pickerell Series
By Ellen MacGregor

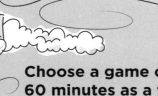

Choose a game or activity to play for 60 minutes as a family or with friends today!

Day 10
Choose a **Play** or **Exercise** Activity!

INCENTIVE CONTRACT CALENDAR

My parents and I agree that if I complete this section of

Summer Fit Activities™

and read _____ minutes a day, my reward will be _____

Child Signature: _____ Parent Signature: _____

Day 1			Day 6		
Day 2			Day 7		
Day 3			Day 8		
Day 4			Day 9		
Day 5			Day 10		

 Color the for each day of activities completed.

 Color the for each day of reading completed.

2-3 • © Summer Fit Activities™

Summer Fitness Log

Choose your exercise activity each day from the Aerobic and Strength Activities in the back of the book. Record the date, stretch, activity and how long you performed your exercise activity below. Fill in how many days you complete your fitness activity on your Incentive Contract Calendars.

	Date	Stretch	Activity	Time
examples:	June 4	Run in place	Sky Reach	7 min
	June 5	Toe Touches	Bottle Curls	15 min
1.				
2.				
3.				
4.				
5.				
6.				
7.				
8.				
9.				
10.				

I promise to do my best for me. I exercise to be healthy and active. I am awesome because I am me.

Child Signature: _____

Picture This

Tell a story about what you might see through a camera lens. Make sure to capitalize the first word of every sentence and to use proper punctuation. Use colorful adjectives and different verbs to tell your story. Illustrate your story in the picture frame.

_____

_____

_____

_____

_____

_____

_____

_____

_____

_____

_____

Addition and Subtraction

1.

35	46	93	41	36
- 18	+ 14	- 35	+ 15	- 14

468	738	253	621	460
- 142	+ 234	+ 236	- 60	+ 243

2. Flower Equations

On each petal write an addition, subtraction, or multiplication equation that equals the number in the center of the flower.

Ex:

Choose your STRENGTH exercise!

Exercise for today:

Day 1

Check & Record in Fitness Log.

2-3 • © Summer Fit Activities™

Alphabetical Order

Number the words in each box to put them in alphabetical order. Choose a word from the word box to describe each group and write in on the line.

fruit	animals	pets	colors	sea life	body parts

Ex: ___Animals___

___4___ monkey

___2___ hippo

___5___ orangutan

___3___ koala

___1___ elephant

1. _____

_____ hamster

_____ dog

_____ bird

_____ cat

_____ rabbit

2. _____

_____ watermelon

_____ pear

_____ banana

_____ apple

_____ orange

3. _____

_____ foot

_____ hand

_____ mouth

_____ eye

_____ nose

4. _____

_____ yellow

_____ green

_____ blue

_____ red

_____ white

5. _____

_____ fish

_____ shark

_____ turtle

_____ dolphin

_____ jellyfish

Write the total for each set.

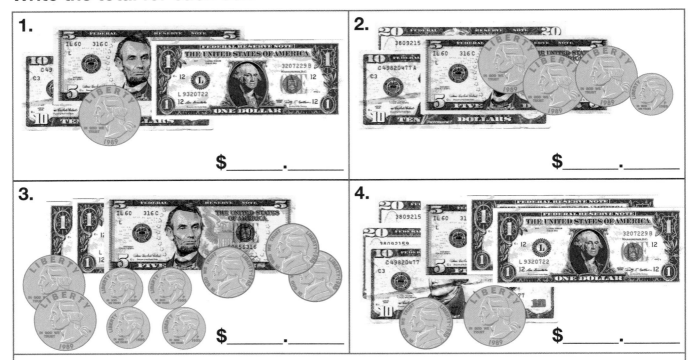

1. $_____._____

2. $_____._____

3. $_____._____

4. $_____._____

5. Draw the bills and coins you would need to buy a bat for $10.00 and a ball for $3.50.

6. Jack has $5.50 and buys a book for $3.50.

How much does he have left? _____

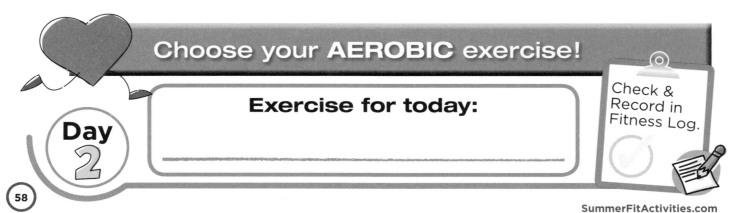

Choose your AEROBIC exercise!

Exercise for today:

Check & Record in Fitness Log.

Day 2

Geography

Use an encyclopedia, library book, atlas or the Internet to look at a world map. Label the continents and oceans and color. Answer the questions below.

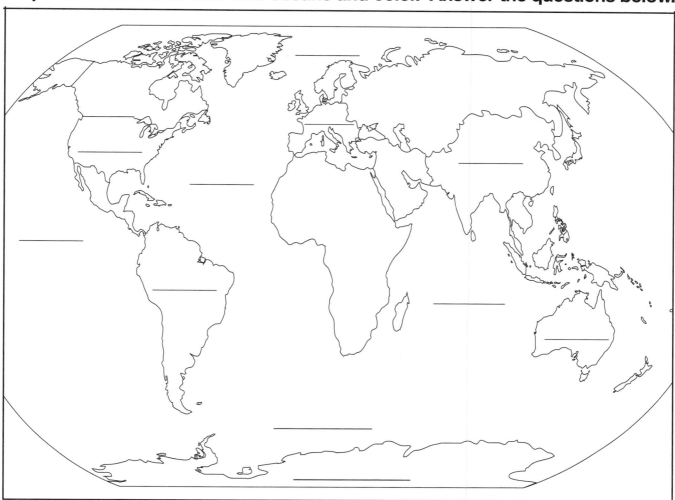

1. How many continents are there?_____

2. Put a star on the continent where you live.

3. How many oceans are there? _____

4. What is the biggest ocean?_____.

5. Draw a red line where the equator is.

Africa
North America
South America
Arctic Ocean
Europe
Atlantic Ocean
Southern Ocean
Indian Ocean
Austrailia
Antarctica
Asia
Pacific Ocean

2-3 • © Summer Fit Activities™

Day 3

Study the menu for Bob's Burger Barn and answer the questions.

Bob's Deluxe Burger............	$3.50	French Fries.........................	$1.50
Cheesy Cheeseburger.........	$3.75	Onion Rings........................	$2.00
Chicken Fingers..................	$4.00	Shake.................................	$3.00
Corn Dog............................	$1.50	Milk, Juice or Soda.............	$1.00
Hot Dog..............................	$1.50	Coffee................................	$0.75

Lucy ordered a cheeseburger, fries and a soda.

1. How much did she spend? _____

2. If Lucy paid with a $10.00 bill how much change did she get back? _____

3. What is the <u>most</u> expensive item on the menu? _____

4. What is the <u>least</u> expensive item on the menu? _____

Choose your STRENGTH exercise!

Exercise for today:

_____

Day 3

Check & Record in Fitness Log.

2-3 • © Summer Fit Activities™

 **Friendly Letter**

Read the friendly letter and label the parts on the line next to it.

Date	Greeting	Body	Closing	Signature

1. _____

2. _____

3. _____

4. _____

5. _____

July 12, 2011

Dear Grandma and Grandpa,

Thank you for the awesome birthday present. A skateboard is just what I wanted! I am having fun riding it at the park with my friends. I'm learning some new tricks and I can't wait to show you.

Your Grandson,

Jon David

Write a friendly letter to someone telling them about your summer.

Make sure to write the date, a greeting, a body, closing and a signature. Include at least 3 things about your summer.

_____

_____

_____

_____

_____

_____

_____

_____

_____

Write the measurement shown by the arrow.

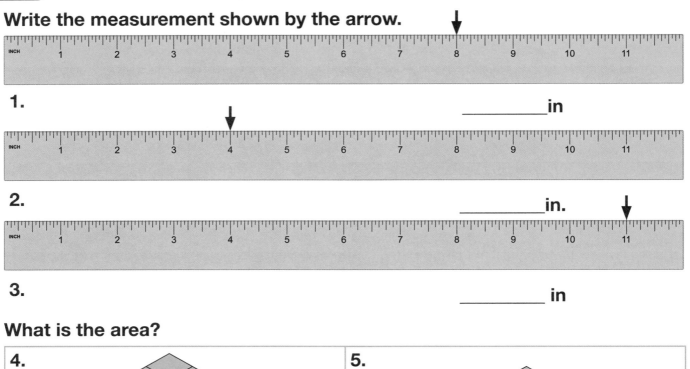

1. _____in

2. _____in.

3. _____ in

What is the area?

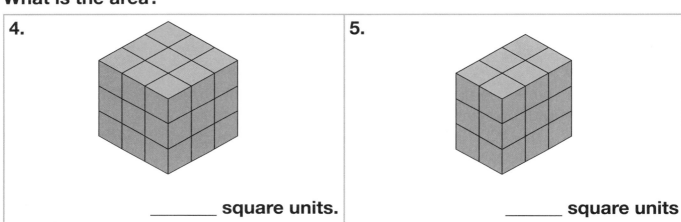

4. _____ square units.

5. _____ square units

6. How many centimeters are in a meter? _____

7. How many feet are in one yard? _____

KINDNESS

Kindness is being nice and caring about other people, animals and the earth. Kindness is looking for ways to understand and help others.

Value

PELE

Pele is from Brazil and is considered by many to be one of the best soccer players to ever play the game. He amazed fans on the soccer field with his awesome plays and many goals. It seemed that no one could stop him! Pele also had a big heart and a big smile. He loved to laugh and make other people feel good. He grew up poor and had to work doing whatever jobs he could to help support his family. He never forgot the lessons he learned or the people who were less fortunate than him. When he retired, Pele dedicated his life to helping others around the world, especially children.

Kindness is caring about others and what happens to them. It is caring about others as much as you care about yourself. Random acts of kindness are kind deeds done for people who aren't expecting it.

Write an act of kindness you could do in each situation.

A mother drops a stack of books at the library so you _____

_____

_____.

A little boy falls off the swing at the playground so you _____

_____

_____.

Your elderly neighbor is feeling sad and lonely so you _____

_____

_____.

Value:

KINDNESS

FAMILY ACTIVITIES

Choose one or more activities to do with your family or friends.

 Play "10 good things" with your friends or family. Pick a person and tell 10 nice things about them.

 Write notes to your neighbors thanking them for being good neighbors.

 Have a lemonade stand and donate the money you earn to a food bank or homeless shelter.

 Collect toys, books, and games you no longer play with and donate them.

Let's talk about it...

Children learn what they live, if they see you practicing random acts of kindness, they will want to do them too. Discuss things your family can do together to help others. Set aside some time to volunteer at a soup kitchen or homeless shelter. Remind your child that kindness begins with a smile and should be practiced at home too!

VALUES ARE A FAMILY AFFAIR

Read more about KINDNESS

City Angel
By Eileen Spinelli

A Chair for My Mother
By Vera B. Williams

Wolf's Favor
By Fulvia Testa

Choose a game or activity to play for 60 minutes as a family or with friends today!

Day 5

Choose a Play or Exercise Activity!

Summer Explorer
Discover New Things to Play and Do!

- Learn how to make paper airplanes.

- Host a board game night.

- Play charades.

- Use cardboard boxes to build an outdoor house, fort, train, or pirate ship.

- Play jump rope, marbles, or hopscotch.

- Use "junk" from around your house to create an art masterpiece.

- Make some puppets and put on a puppet show.

- Go through your toys and have a toy exchange or donate to charity.

- Fly a kite.

- Draw with sidewalk or paint with water on the cement.

- Create a new exercise or exercise routine.

- Organize a neighborhood garbage walk to pick up trash and clean up your neighborhood.

- Search for animal tracks. How many can you identify?

- Play in the sand. Build a sand castle.

- Play Frisbee.

- Write a letter to someone and mail it.

- Visit a local nature preserve.

- Make a robot or other creation out of items from your recycle bin.

- Paint a pet rock.

Recyclable Creations "Junk Monsters"

 Gather clean cans, bottles, and boxes from recycling bin.

 Use plastic lids, newspaper strips, nuts, screws, buttons, pipe cleaners, rubber bands to make faces, and arms and legs. Your parents will need to help you glue with a hot glue gun.

 Create monsters, robots, or your family members!

Summer Journal III

Write about your best friend, brother or sister.

2-3 • © Summer Fit Activities™

Possessive Nouns

A possessive noun shows ownership. Add an 's to each singular noun to make it possessive.

The dog that belongs to my brother. My _____brother's_____ dog.

Ex:

1. The lyrics of the song. The _____ lyrics.

2. The cake that is for Sam. _____cake.

3. The nest of the bird. The _____nest.

Add 's to singular nouns and ' after the s of the plural nouns.

Ex: **shoes**   **shoes'**   **7. snake**   _____

4. teacher   _____   **8. mom**   _____

5. boy   _____   **9. singers**   _____

6. parents   _____   **10. king**   _____

1. Write the number that comes before and after by 10s.

Ex. __55__ _65_ _75___   _____35_____   _____60_____

_____20_____   _____45_____   _____100____

Place Value. Read the words and write the correct value in the blank.

2.

35 = _____ tens _____ ones   98 = _____ tens _____ ones

44 = _____ tens _____ ones   75 = _____ tens _____ ones

11 = _____ tens _____ ones   54 = _____ tens _____ ones

3.

7 tens 5 ones = _____   3 tens 3 ones = _____

9 tens 2 ones = _____   4 tens 1 ones = _____

Choose your AEROBIC exercise!

Exercise for today:

_____

Day 6

Check & Record in Fitness Log.

2-3 • © Summer Fit Activities™

Mind Your Manners!

A syllable is the sound of a vowel (a, e, i, o, u) that you hear when saying a word out loud.

Say the following words out loud while clapping your hands to count out how many syllables each word has.

Ex: **marching band** ___3___   drum _____

trombone _____   bassoon _____

clarinet _____   flute _____

guitar _____   tuba _____

Beethoven _____   instrument _____

musician _____   band _____

saxophone _____   trumpet _____

Mixed Practice

Write the numbers.

1. Six hundred thirty two _____

2. Five hundred seventy one _____

3. Nine hundred sixty five _____

4. Three hundred ninety _____

5. One hundred four _____

Add or Subtract.

6. 800 – 300 = _____   7. 200 + 400 = _____   8. 600 – 200 = _____

9. 300 + 500 = _____   10. 400 – 100 = _____   11. 700 – 400 = _____

Write <,>,=

12. 20 + 20 _____ 30 + 10   13. 12 + 7 _____ 17 – 1

14. 30 + 15 – 10 _____ 40 – 15 + 5   15. 3 + 9 + 10 _____ 4 + 8

Choose your STRENGTH exercise!

Day 7

Exercise for today:

_____

Check & Record in Fitness Log.

2-3 • © Summer Fit Activities™

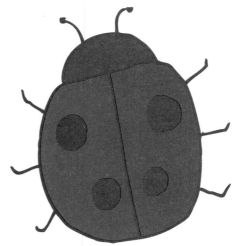

The ladybug is a gardener's friend. Ladybugs are helpful because they eat pests in the garden. One ladybug can eat 50 aphids a day! Like all insects, the ladybug has six legs, three body parts, and a pair of antennae. The ladybug's hard outer wings protect the transparent wings underneath that are used for flying.

In the spring the ladybug lays its eggs on a leaf where there are plenty of aphids nearby. When the eggs hatch, the tiny black larvae that emerge don't look anything like ladybugs. The young larvae eat and grow until it is time to change into a ladybug. The larva attaches itself to a leaf and the old skin splits off. Inside the pupa a ladybug is forming. After about a week the soft, yellow ladybug pushes its way out of the shell. Soon the outer wings harden and turn red with black spots. Some birds think the brightly colored ladybug would be good to eat but the yellow liquid they excrete makes them taste terrible! Most ladybugs hibernate during the winter. They huddle together in a warm, safe place until the cold winter months are over. When spring arrives the hungry ladybugs begin their search for food.

1. Ladybugs are helpful because they eat _____.

2. Ladybugs have _____ body parts and _____ legs.

3. Ladybugs are born yellow with no _____.

4. Most ladybugs hibernate during the _____.

5. Ladybugs taste _____ to birds.

1. What are the even numbers: _____,_____,_____,_____,_____

2. What is the sum of the even numbers? _____

3. Write the odd numbers:_____,_____,_____,_____,_____

4. What is the sum of the odd numbers?_____

5. What are three numbers that add up to 15? ____ + _____ + _____ = 15

6. What is the largest number? _____

7. What odd number is greater than 5 but less than 9? _____

8. Two times this number is 4 _____

Choose your AEROBIC exercise!

Exercise for today:

_____

Check & Record in Fitness Log.

Day 8

Choose the correct homophone for each sentence and write it on the line.

1. An _____ bit my toe.

   Aunt, ant

2. My _____ Lucy took me to a movie.

   Aunt, ant

3. My birthday is in one _____.

   week, weak

4. The calf was too _____ to stand on its own.

   week, weak

5. I will _____ my grandparents a letter.

   right, write

6. I am _____ handed.

   right, write

7. We _____ hot dogs and peanuts at the baseball game.

   eight, ate

8. There are _____ people in my family.

   eight, ate

9. Remember to _____ sunscreen when you go swimming.

   wear, where

10. Do you know _____ your parents were born?

    wear, where

11. I ate an apple and a _____ for breakfast.

    pear, pair

12. My Grandma sent me a new _____ of shoes for my birthday.

    pair, pear

What is the area?

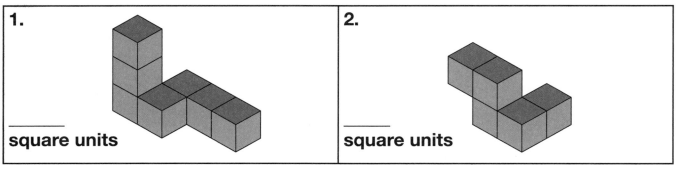

1. _____ square units

2. _____ square units

Draw a line 4 inches.

Look at each pair of shapes. Write how it was moved.

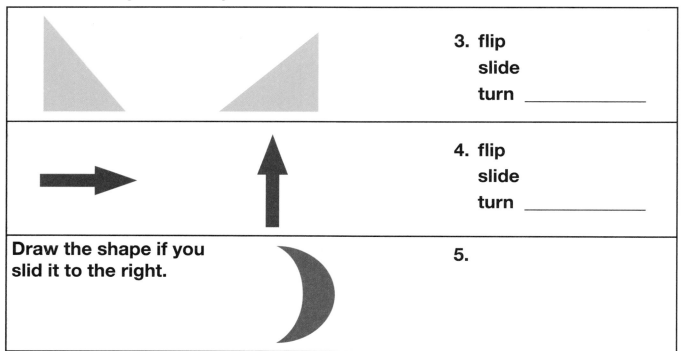

3. flip

slide

turn _____

4. flip

slide

turn _____

Draw the shape if you slid it to the right.

5.

Choose your **STRENGTH** exercise!

Exercise for today:

Check & Record in Fitness Log.

Day 9

COURAGE

Courage means doing the right thing even when you are feeling scared.

Rosa Parks

Rosa Parks was one of the heroes of the Civil Rights Movement in the United States of America. Before the Civil Rights Movement, African-Americans were not treated well. They had to sit in the back of busses and even had to give up their seat to white people. One day after work, Rosa got on the bus to go home. When the bus driver told Rosa to give up her seat for a white man she refused. Rosa showed courage by standing up for what was right even though she was afraid.

As a family, watch a movie that demonstrates courage such as *Charlotte's Web, The Sound of Music, The Wizard of Oz, The Lion King, ET,* or *Finding Nemo.*

Discuss how the characters in the movie display courage. What might have happened if they hadn't been courageous?

Name a movie you watched that showed courage.

_____

How did the characters show courage? _____

_____

_____

_____

_____

_____.

Value: COURAGE

FAMILY ACTIVITIES

Choose one or more activities to do with your family or friends.

 As a family, watch a movie that demonstrates courage such as *Charlotte's Web*, *The Sound of Music*, *The Wizard of Oz*, *The Lion King*, *ET*, or *Finding Nemo*. Discuss how the characters in the movie display courage. What might have happened if they hadn't been courageous?

 Make and decorate a pennant for your room that says "I believe in myself." Discuss with your parents how being the best you can be is an act of courage.

 Talk about the courage it takes for a blind person to get through the day. Take turns blindfolding each other and try to do your everyday things. Ask your parents to help you look up the story of Ben Underwood, a blind teen who rides a skateboard and plays video games.

 Think about the most courageous person you know. Write about how they demonstrate courage.

Let's talk about it...

Courage is something built over time. Discuss everyday situations with your child and the opportunities they have to be brave. Read books about people who display courage. Encourage them to share their fears and brainstorm together ways to face and overcome those fears. Talk with them about a time you were afraid but found the courage to get through.

VALUES ARE A FAMILY AFFAIR

Read more about COURAGE

The Courage of Sarah Noble
By Alice Dalgliesh

Abel's Island
By William Steig

Call It Courage
By Armstrong Sperry

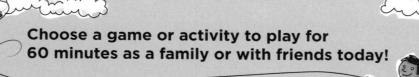

Choose a game or activity to play for 60 minutes as a family or with friends today!

Day 10

Choose a Play or Exercise Activity!

INCENTIVE CONTRACT CALENDAR

My parents and I agree that if I complete this section of

Summer Fit Activities™

and read _____ minutes a day, my reward will be _____

Child Signature: _____   Parent Signature: _____

Day 1			Day 6		
Day 2			Day 7		
Day 3			Day 8		
Day 4			Day 9		
Day 5			Day 10		

Color the for each day of activities completed.

Color the for each day of reading completed.

Summer Fitness Log

Choose your exercise activity each day from the Aerobic and Strength Activities in the back of the book. Record the date, stretch, activity and how long you performed your exercise activity below. Fill in how many days you complete your fitness activity on your Incentive Contract Calendars.

	Date	Stretch	Activity	Time
examples:	June 4	Run in place	Sky Reach	7 min
	June 5	Toe Touches	Bottle Curls	15 min
1.				
2.				
3.				
4.				
5.				
6.				
7.				
8.				
9.				
10.				

I promise to do my best for me. I exercise to be healthy and active. I am awesome because I am me.

Child Signature: _____

Pronouns are words that replace nouns. Choose a pronoun to replace the underlined word or words.

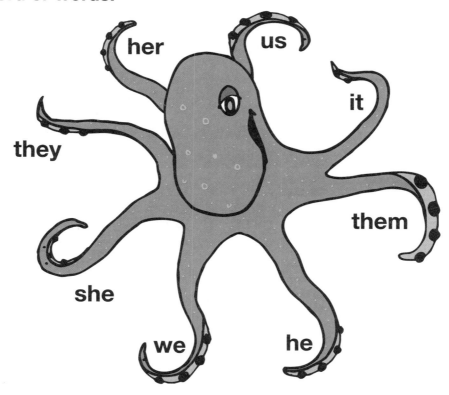

her us

it

they

them

she

we he

1. I asked <u>Mom</u> to bake me a cake. _____

2. <u>Coach</u> <u>Dan</u> is my baseball coach. _____

3. <u>Maddie</u> and <u>Grace</u> are twins. _____

4. <u>Sam</u>, <u>Felix</u> and <u>I</u> are going to the movies. _____

5. I hit the <u>ball</u> across the field. _____

6. Adam went to the waterpark with <u>Milo</u>, <u>Josh</u>, and <u>me</u>. _____

7. <u>Mary</u> is my babysitter. _____

8. I will go with <u>Grandma</u> and <u>Grandpa</u> to the park. _____

Number Riddles.

My hundreds digit is 6. My tens digit is 2 less than 4. The digit in the ones place is 1 more than my hundreds digit.

1. What number am I? _____

You will get my hundreds digit when you double 4. Subtract 2 from my hundreds digit to get my tens digit. My ones digit is 3 more than my tens digit.

2. What number am I? _____

My hundreds digit is 4 x 1. My tens digit is 3 x 2. The digit in the ones place is the tens digit + 3.

3. What number am I?_____

4. Use the numbers above, list in order from smallest to largest.

_____, _____, _____

Choose your STRENGTH exercise!

Exercise for today:

_____

Day 1

Check & Record in Fitness Log.

 **Matter**

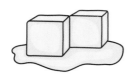  

Matter is anything that takes up space. Everything in our world is made up of matter. Matter can take three different forms: solid, liquid and gas. Each form has different qualities that make it a solid, liquid, or gas. Solids have a definite shape while liquids and gasses take the shape of the container they are in.

After each word write S if it is a solid, L if it is a liquid, and G if it is a gas.

1. water _____   4. smoke _____   7. air _____   10. book _____

2. ice _____   5. milk _____   8. desk _____   11. soda _____

3. helium _____   6. wood _____   9. steam _____   12. syrup _____

Liquid or solid? Make flubber and see if it is a solid or a liquid or both.

What you need:
Borax
white glue
water
sticks for stirring
Food coloring
2 bowls

Instructions:
In bowl 1, dissolve 2 bottles of glue in warm (very warm) water, add several drops of food coloring. In bowl 2, dissolve 1 and ½ tsp. Borax into 1 cup warm water. Slowly pour Borax mixture into glue mixture, stir until combined and have fun!

The atmosphere surrounding Earth is full of air! Air is a mixture of gasses that we need to live — it is everywhere! On a separate sheet of paper, draw some places where you find air.

Add or subtract. Color the spiders with even answers gray,
color spiders with odd answers brown.

Count by 3's to finish the pattern. Circle all the even numbers.

3, _____, _____, _____, _____, _____, _____, _____, _____, _____, _____, 36.

Choose your **AEROBIC** exercise!

Exercise for today:

Day 2

Check & Record in Fitness Log.

2-3 • © Summer Fit Activities™

SummerFitActivities.com

Beginning Blends and Digraphs

Write the beginning blend for each picture on the line.

_____	_____	_____	_____	_____	_____
_____	_____	_____	_____	_____	_____
_____	_____	_____	_____	_____	_____
_____	_____	_____	_____	_____	_____

Numbers and Math - Mixed Practice

It's a rat race! Multiply by 3 to help the rat get to the cheese.

3 x 1 = __**3**__

3 x 4 = _____

3 x 2 = _____

3 x 0 = _____

3 x 6 = _____

3 x 7 = _____

3 x 10 = _____

3 x 9 = _____

3 x 8 = _____

3 x 5 = _____

3 x 11 = _____

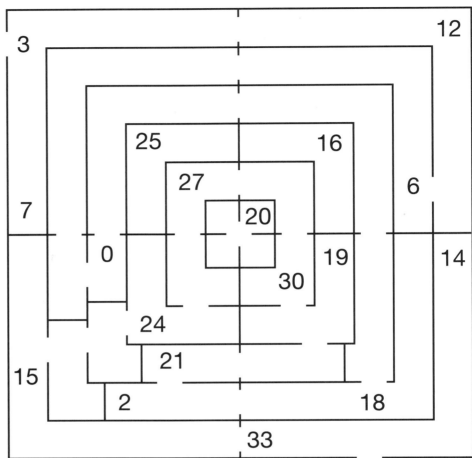

Divide the 18 spiders into groups of 3. How many groups of 3 are there?

18 ÷ 3 = _____

Choose your STRENGTH exercise!

Day 3

Exercise for today:
_____

Check & Record in Fitness Log.

 **Make it Right**

Circle the mistakes and write the letter correctly in your best handwriting.

May 13 2014

dear alex

    we are going camping on june 10th.   would you like to come with us
we re going to go fishing and make s'mores please let me no if you can come it
will be a lot of fun

your friend

josh

_____

_____

_____

_____

_____

_____

_____

_____

The Thunderbolts had a great soccer season. Study the chart of goals made for the first 6 games and answer the questions below.

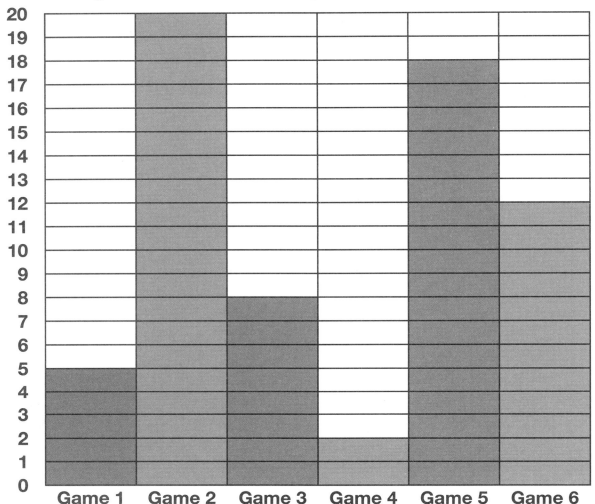

1. In which game were the most goals scored? _____
2. How many goals were scored in Game 2? _____
3. Which game had the least amount of goals scored? _____
4. How many more goals were scored in Game 5 than Game 1? ____
5. What was the total number of goals scored for Games 1-6? _____

Choose your AEROBIC exercise!

Exercise for today:

Check & Record in Fitness Log.

Day 4

2-3 • © Summer Fit Activities™

SummerFitActivities.com

RESPECT

Respect is honoring yourself and others. It is behaving in a way that makes life peaceful and orderly.

Mahatma Gandhi, whose name means "Great Soul," was a great political and spiritual leader of India. For years he helped people stand up against unfair treatment through peaceful protests, marches, and strikes. Gandhi believed that every life was valuable and worthy of respect. He worked hard to improve the rights of the poor, women, and workers in his country.

Gandhi taught that if you hurt another you are really hurting yourself. He taught peace over power and encouraged everyone to find ways to get along and live in harmony with love and respect for all.

Synonyms are words that mean the same thing. Draw a line to match each word with its synonym.

1. justice   admiration

2. harmony   freedom

3. respect   fairness

4. independence   peace

Value: RESPECT

Respect is showing good manners and acceptance of other people and our planet. Respect is celebrating differences in culture, ideas and experiences that are different than yours. Respect is accepting that others have lessons to teach us because of their experiences.

> "Be the change you want to see in the world."
>
> - Mahatma Gandhi

List 3 ways to show respect to your parents and teachers.

1 _____

2 _____

3 _____

We can disrespect people with our words. Remember to THINK before we speak. Ask yourself...

T = is it true?

H = Is it helpful or hurtful?

I = Is it inspiring?

N = Is it necessary?

K = Is it kind?

WAYS TO SHOW RESPECT

Respect the Earth.
Collect items to recycle.

Respect a different culture:
Listen to some music or try a new food that is associated with a culture or belief that is different than yours.

Day 5 Choose a **Play** or **Exercise Activity!**

Summer Explorer
Discover New Things to Play and Do!

- Learn the phases of the moon. Look at it several nights in a row and see if you can recognize the various phases.

- Make up a song or dance.

- Have a yard sale.

- Start a rock collection.

- Have a potluck with family and friends.

- Visit a farmers market. Learn about the origin of the food you eat.

- Volunteer.

- Take a hike.

- Have a neighborhood softball game.

- Make popsicles.

- Grab some binoculars and go on a bird watching hike.

- Go camping.

- Have a western theme night. Wear bandannas and your cowboy boots, and roast hotdogs. Try line dancing or watch an old Western.

- Go on a nature walk. Collect twigs, leaves, pebbles, and shells. Glue them on card stock to make a 3D masterpiece.

- Help a neighbor by mowing their lawn or weeding.

- Draw a comic strip.

- Bake cookies and take some to a friend or neighbor.

- Play Hide and Seek.

- Have a pillow fight.

- Create a time capsule.

Nature Walk

 Go on a nature walk in a field, park or beach.

 Collect grass, twigs, shells, pebbles, etc.

 Arrange your finds inside a cardboard box, glue down to create a 3D masterpiece.

2-3 • © Summer Fit Activities™

Summer Journal IV

Write about your best summer day so far.

 **All Jumbled Up**

Unscramble the sentences so they make sense and rewrite them on the line. Remember to capitalize and add punctuation.

1. rode I my bike to sunset park

_____

2. the zoo saw we monkeys at

_____

3. soccer I have wednesday practice on.

_____

4. and I my sister made cookies for grandma.

_____

5. you like do collect to stamps

_____

6. flowers the we in planted the spring blooming. now are

_____

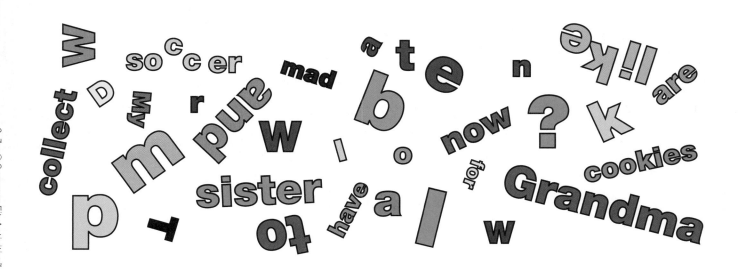

How many bills and coins do you need for each total?

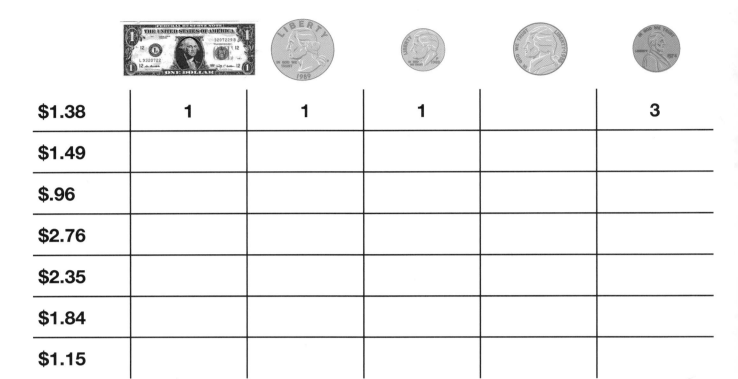

$1.38	1	1	1		3
$1.49					
$.96					
$2.76					
$2.35					
$1.84					
$1.15					

Count by 4s.

4, _____, _____, _____, _____, _____, _____, _____, _____, 40

George has 16 gum balls. If he gives each of his 4 friends the same number of gum balls, how many does each friend get?

_____

Choose your AEROBIC exercise!

Exercise for today:

Check & Record in Fitness Log.

Day 6

Robin's Secret

We have a secret, just we three,
The robin, and I, and the sweet cherry tree;
The bird told the tree, and the tree told me,
And nobody knows but just we three.
Of course, the robin knows it best,
Because it built the- I shan't tell the rest;
And laid the four little—somethings in it;
I'm afraid I shall tell it this very minute.
But if the tree and the robins don't peep,
I'll try my best the secret to keep;
Though I know, when the little birds fly about;
Then the whole secret will be out.

1. What kind of bird is mentioned in this poem? _____

2. What did the bird build in the tree? _____

3. What kind of tree? _____

4. What are the four little "somethings"? _____

5. What word in the poem rhymes with peep? _____

6. What word rhymes with about? _____

7. What is the secret the poem is talking about? _____

8. Circle all the contractions in this poem.

How long is each critter?

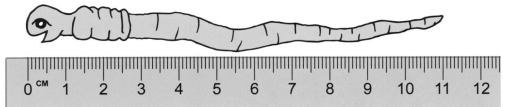

1. _____ cm

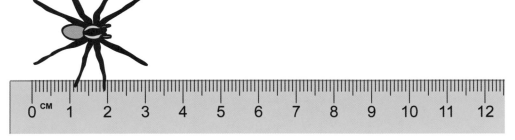

2. _____ cm

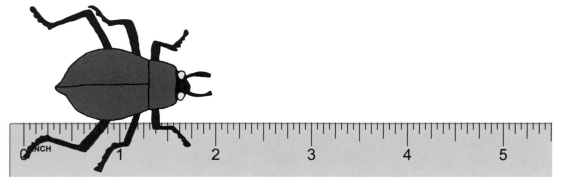

3. _____ in

4. _____ in

Day 7

Choose your STRENGTH exercise!

Exercise for today:

_____

Check & Record in Fitness Log.

 **Ending Blends**

Write the name of each picture. Circle the consonant blend that makes the ending sound.

1. MILK _____	**2.** _____	**3.** _____	**4.** _____
5. _____	**6.** _____	**7.** _____	**8.** _____

Say each word and circle the consonant digraph.

Ex: 9. (wheel)	10. school	11. brother	12. gnaw
13. mother	14. rough	15. nickel	16. shake
17. telephone	18. wrist	19. knit	20. know
21. thick	22. peaches	23. tooth	24. cheese
25. thought	26. write	27. push	28. farther
29. cherry	30. duck	31. laugh	32. elephant

Story Problems

Read and answer. Show how you got your answer.

1. There are 9 kids on the baseball team. If each player makes 2 home runs,

how many home runs will the team have? _____

_____

2. A quart of milk equals 4 cups. If Joan needs 3 quarts of milk to make

homemade ice cream, how many cups of milk will she use? _____

_____

3. The Roberts family ordered 4 pizzas. If there are 10 slices in each pizza, how

many slices will they have in all? _____

_____

4. How much money does Carlos have? $ _____

$ _____

**Does he have enough to buy a squirt gun that costs $4.00? If not, how
much more money does he need?**

_____

**5. It is 3:00 when Isabelle goes to dance class. If her dance class
is 45 minutes long, what time will it be when class is over?**

_____

Draw the hands on the clock to show the time.

Choose your **AEROBIC** exercise!

Day 8

Exercise for today:

_____

Check &
Record in
Fitness Log.

The Story of Your Tongue

Read the story and answer the questions.

Your sense of taste comes from your tongue. Look closely in the mirror while you stick out your tongue. The little bumps you see are your taste buds. When you eat, the nerves inside your taste buds send a message to your brain that tells it what you are eating.

There are taste buds for each different kind of taste: salty, sweet, sour, and bitter. Each part of your tongue has a job for tasting food. The tip of your tongue tastes things that are sweet while the back of your tongue tastes things that are bitter. The sides of your tongue taste salty and sour food.

Try to "trick" your tongue. Put some sugar on the back of your tongue. How long does it take for you to taste the sweetness of the sugar? Try putting something bitter on the tip of your tongue. Do you taste the bitterness right away?

Fill in the blanks with words from the passage above to answer the questions.

1. **The bumps you see at the back of your tongue are**

_____ _____.

2. **Your taste buds send a message to your**

_____ **to tell it what you are eating.**

3. **The four kinds of tastes are:**

_____, _____,

_____, and _____.

4. **The tip of your tongue tastes**

_____.

5. **The sides of your tongue tastes salty and** _____ **foods.**

6. **Can you name something that tastes salty?** _____

7. **Can you name something that tastes sour?** _____

8. **Bitter?** _____ **Sweet?** _____

Fill in the blanks.

1. 1 yd. = _____ in.	2. 12 in. = _____ ft.	3. 1 hour = _____ min.
4. 3 ft. = _____ yd.	5. 1 day = _____ hr.	6. 36 in. = _____ yd.

7. Use a ruler to draw a line to these lengths.
The starting point is drawn for you.

3 inches •

1 ½ inches •

2 inches •

½ inches •

8. **Write the number of ones, tens, hundreds, and thousands in the following numbers. Say each number.**

	Thousands	Hundreds	Tens	Ones
8,965				
4,640				
9,027				
5,932				

Choose your STRENGTH exercise!

Exercise for today:

_____

Day 9

Check & Record in Fitness Log.

Value

Responsibility is to do what you think you should, for yourself and others, even when it is difficult.

Terrance Stanley Fox was a very good athlete. His favorite sport was basketball but he also played rugby, golf and ran cross country in high school. Sadly, Terry lost one of his legs because he got cancer, but he felt it was his responsibility to do all that he could for other people with cancer. Even though it was very hard, he set off to run across Canada with an artificial leg to raise money for cancer research. He called his run the Marathon of Hope. When he started to run not many people knew about Terry or what he was doing. Today people all over the world participate or take part in an event named after Terry to raise money for cancer research.

Synonyms are words that mean the same thing. Draw a line to match each word with its synonym.

1. hard   named

2. began   earned

3. raised   difficult

4. called   started

Value: RESPONSIBILITY

You can show responsibility in many different ways. From doing your homework to babysitting your little brother or sister to helping someone else who is in need, being responsible is being accountable for your actions. Big and small, choosing what you do with your time and efforts is an important part of being responsible.

> "I am not doing the run to become rich or famous."
>
> - Terry Fox, *Marathon of Hope*

Monday	
Tuesday	
Wednesday	
Thursday	
Friday	
Saturday	
Sunday	

Build or set up a bird feeder in your yard and be responsible for feeding the birds. Use the chart below to track how many birds you feed for a week.

We are all responsible for the environment. Watch one of these family movies and talk about how being irresponsible can affect the environment. Movies: *Over the Hedge, Hoot, Free Willy, Bambi, Fern Gully, The Last Rainforest,* or *Happy Feet*.

Day 10

Choose a Play or Exercise Activity!

2–3 • © Summer Fit Activities™

INCENTIVE CONTRACT CALENDAR

My parents and I agree that if I complete this section of

Summer Fit Activities™

and read _____ minutes a day, my reward will be _____

Child Signature: _____   Parent Signature: _____

Day 1			Day 6		
Day 2			Day 7		
Day 3			Day 8		
Day 4			Day 9		
Day 5			Day 10		

 Color the for each day of activities completed.

 Color the for each day of reading completed.

Summer Fitness Log

Choose your exercise activity each day from the Aerobic and Strength Activities in the back of the book. Record the date, stretch, activity and how long you performed your exercise activity below. Fill in how many days you complete your fitness activity on your Incentive Contract Calendars.

	Date	Stretch	Activity	Time
examples:	June 4	Run in place	Sky Reach	7 min
	June 5	Toe Touches	Bottle Curls	15 min
1.				
2.				
3.				
4.				
5.				
6.				
7.				
8.				
9.				
10.				

I promise to do my best for me. I exercise to be healthy and active. I am awesome because I am me.

Child Signature: _____

Table of Contents

There are many parts of a book. The Table of Contents is at the beginning of the book. It tells you the names and pages of each chapter. Study this Table of Contents from a book called The Human Body then answer the questions below.

1. In which chapter would you read about how your lungs work? _____

2. Which chapter would tell you about the nervous system? _____

3. What page does the chapter about your heart begin? _____

4. What is chapter 11 about? _____

5. Which chapter would tell you about how your body digests its food?

_____

6. What pages would you read to learn about your brain? _____

7. On a separate piece of paper, draw a picture of what the cover of this book might look like.

1. Solve these multiplication problems.

3 x 2		8 x 3		0 x 5		4 x 4		6 x 10	
4 x 2		4 x 3		1 x 5		2 x 4		4 x 10	
5 x 2		2 x 3		4 x 5		0 x 4		1 x 10	
7 x 2		5 x 3		6 x 5		1 x 4		8 x 10	
1 x 2		1 x 3		5 x 5		3 x 4		2 x 10	

2. Round each number to the nearest 100.

569 _____   120 _____   349 _____

798 _____   637 _____   289 _____

201 _____   876 _____   456 _____

Choose your STRENGTH exercise!

Exercise for today:

_____

Day 1

Check & Record in Fitness Log.

"Y" can make the long i sound and the long e sound when it is the only vowel at the end of a syllable. Say the words and listen for the "y" sound. Write each word in the correct column.

family	cry	library	sunny	sky	why	puppy
shy	lady	try	baby	fly	penny	reply

Y = long i

_____

_____

_____

_____

_____

_____

_____

Y = long e

_____

_____

_____

_____

_____

_____

_____

Find a word from the box above to complete each sentence and write it on the line.

1. We like to check out books from the _____.

2. There are nine people in my _____.

3. I like to play with my _____ brother.

4. It was a _____ day so I wore my sunglasses.

5. I can _____ my kite on a windy day.

Data Management: Calendar

Use the calendar to answer the following questions.

July						
Sunday	**Monday**	**Tuesday**	**Wednesday**	**Thursday**	**Friday**	**Saturday**
	1	2	3	4	5	6
7	8	9	10	11	12	13
14	15	16	17	18	19	20
21	22	23	24	25	26	27
28	29	30	31			

1. How many Mondays are in the month of July? _____

2. Name the date three weeks from July 3rd. _____

3. What day of the week is July 18th? _____

4. What is the date of the 4th Saturday in July? _____

5. How many Fridays in the month of July? _____

6. What day of the week is the last day of the month? _____

7. Write the abbreviation for the months of the year.

January	_____	July	_____
February	_____	August	_____
March	_____	September	_____
April	_____	October	_____
May	_____	November	_____
June	_____	December	_____

Choose your AEROBIC exercise!

Exercise for today:

_____

Check & Record in Fitness Log.

Day 2

2-3 • © Summer Fit Activities™

Habitats

A habitat is a place where plants and animals live. A habitat provides what plants and animals need to survive and thrive. Some of the things plants and animals need are air, food, water, light, and space. There are many different habitats on Earth.

Draw a line from the picture of the habitat to its name.

Forest	Desert	Pond

(cactus, snake, sun)	(water, reeds, frog)	(pine tree,deer)

Write the plants and animals that might live in each habitat.

____________________	____________________	____________________
____________________	____________________	____________________
____________________	____________________	____________________

What is the main idea of the paragraph at the top of the page?

____

____

____

____

Look at the grid. The * is on A, 2 . Follow the directions for each location.

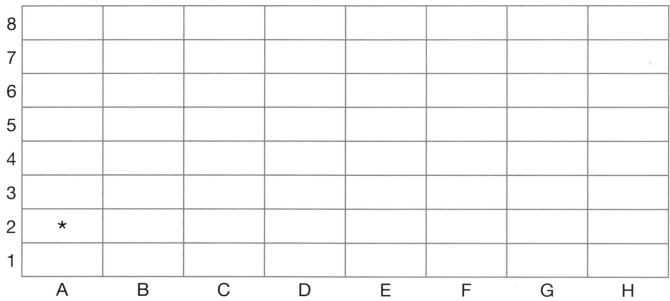

Draw a red heart in B, 3.

Put an x on D, 7.

Draw a line from C, 6 to F, 6.

Put a black dot in H, 1.

Color the square at F, 5 yellow.

Draw a green star in A, 8.

Color half of G, 4 orange.

Add:

590	723	645
+ 125	+ 275	+ 232

 Choose your STRENGTH exercise!

Day 3

Exercise for today:
_____

 Check & Record in Fitness Log.

Write the numbers 1-5 to put these sentences in order.

1.

_____ A tadpole hatches from the egg.

_____ The tadpole's tail gets smaller while its legs begin to grow.

_____ A tadpole forms inside the egg.

_____ The tail is gone and the tadpole is now a frog.

_____ A frog lays an egg in the pond.

2.

_____ The flower blooms.

_____ A plant sprouts.

_____ The seed gets water deep in the ground.

_____ A seed is planted.

_____ The plant gets taller and a flower begins to bud.

A line: goes without end in both directions.

A ray: has one endpoint and goes without end in one direction.

A line segment: has two endpoints.

Circle the correct name.

1. ⟷	line	ray	line segment
2. •⟶	line	ray	line segment
3. •—•	line	ray	line segment

4. Look at the angles. Circle all the right angles.

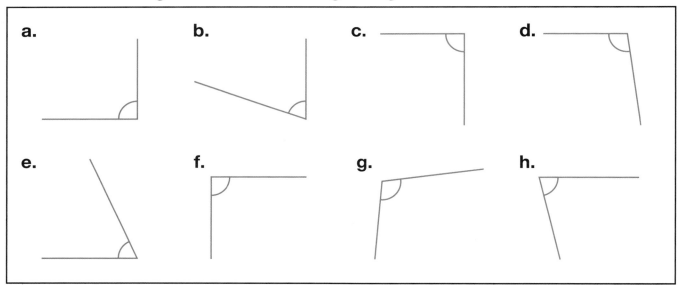

Choose your AEROBIC exercise!

Exercise for today:

Check & Record in Fitness Log.

Day 4

110

2-3 • © Summer Fit Activities™

SummerFitActivities.com

PERSEVERANCE

Value

Perseverance is not giving up or giving in when things are difficult. It means you try again when you fail.

Shark Attack!

Bethany Hamilton was sitting on her surfboard one sunny day in Hawaii, waiting for the next big wave. Before she knew what had happened, a tiger shark attacked and she was left without one arm. Thirteen-year old Bethany almost died but she survived and was soon back in the water surfing again. Bethany had to overcome her fear of another shark attack and had to teach herself how to surf with only one arm. Little by little, she worked at it until she was soon surfing again and winning competitions.

Look up the following words in the dictionary and write what they mean.

Disability: _____

_____

_____

_____

_____.

Obstacles: _____

_____

_____

_____

_____.

Value: PERSEVERANCE

FAMILY ACTIVITIES

Choose one or more activities to do with your family or friends.

 As a family, tackle a big job you have been putting off such as cleaning the garage or painting the fence. Work together as a family to persevere and finish the job. Celebrate with ice cream to emphasize the sweet satisfaction of a job well done.

 People with disabilities face many obstacles each day. Read about Helen Keller and her perseverance in overcoming her blindness and deafness. Put on a blindfold and imagine how hard it would be to go about your day without your sight. What can you do? What can't you do?

 Farmers need perseverance and a lot of patience when planting their crops. One bad storm or drought can destroy everything they have worked for. Plant a small vegetable garden and take care of weeding and watering it. Be patient and your perseverance will pay off.

VALUES ARE A FAMILY AFFAIR

Read more about PERSEVERANCE

The Iditarod: Story of the Last Great Race
By Ian Young

Hugh Can Do
By Jennifer Armstrong

Mandela
By Floyd Cooper

Choose a game or activity to play for 60 minutes as a family or with friends today!

Day 5

Choose a **Play** or **Exercise** Activity!

Summer Explorer
Discover New Things to Play and Do!

- Make up a secret handshake.

- Play "I spy".

- Write a poem.

- Make a telescope out of paper towel tubes. Have a family stargazing night: How many constellations can you find? Can you find the Big Dipper? Polaris?

- Do a puzzle.

- Make ice cream.

- Make a friendship bracelet and give it to a friend.

- Learn to fold Origami.

- Go fishing.

- Camp in the backyard.

- Learn how to juggle.

- Feed the ducks.

- Turn on some music and dance.

- Hang butcher paper on a wall and paint a mural.

- Learn the alphabet in sign language.

- Learn Pig Latin.

- Host a tea party.

- Have a Super Hero Day - dress like your favorite super hero or make up your own. Dress up your pet!

- Walk a dog.

- Do a science experiment.

- Pretend you are a reporter. Interview someone special and write an article about him/her.

Stargazing

 Collect paper towel tubes.

 Gather your family on a clear night to stargaze through your "telescopes".

 Look for The Big Dipper, Cancer and other star constellations.

Summer Journal V

Write about your favorite pet or animal.

Nouns can be common nouns or proper nouns. A proper noun names a specific person, place, or thing. Proper nouns should be capitalized and can include the names of people, cities, months, and states, geographical areas, books, and sometimes things. Underline all the nouns, print a capital letter for the proper nouns which should be capitalized.

D   F
1. **Ex:** Our <u>family</u> went to <u>disneyworld</u> in <u>florida</u>.

albert einstein was a famous physicist.

We went to pizza palace for my brother tom's birthday.

My friend mary works at the evergreen library.

yellowstone park is a great place to go camping in june.

The grand canyon is located in arizona.

2. Think of a proper noun for each common noun given.

common noun	proper noun
lake	The Great Salt Lake
state	_____
book	_____
park	_____
person	_____
store	_____
ocean	_____
restaurant	_____

1. Multiply Quickly.

4 x 4 = _____   5 x 3 = _____   2 x 4 = _____

3 x 2 = _____   6 x 1 = _____   4 x 0 = _____

4 x 5 = _____   2 x 4 = _____   2 x 2 = _____

3 x 4 = _____   6 x 3 = _____   2 x 6 = _____

1 x 4 = _____   5 x 0 = _____   3 x 3 = _____

2. Read the clues to solve the riddle.

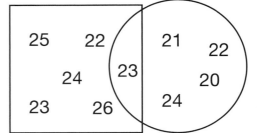

I am not in the square.

I am less than 22.

I am an even number. I am _____.

Solve.

3. (3 + 2) x (10 − 6) = _____   4. (10 - 8) + (15 x 1) = _____

5. Six + five + ten − 21 = _____   6. 25 − 5 − 10 - 2 = _____

Choose your AEROBIC exercise!

Exercise for today:

Check & Record in Fitness Log.

Day 6

2-3 • © Summer Fit Activities™

Thoughts of a Third Grader

Write a few sentences to describe each activity. Use descriptive words (adjectives), exciting action words (verbs), and give a lot of detail. Use your writing to help the reader experience the sights, sounds, and smells of what you are describing.

Riding a roller coaster at an amusement park.

_____

_____

_____

_____

Eating cotton candy at the fair.

_____

_____

_____

_____

Visiting a bakery.

_____

_____

_____

_____

Swimming in the ocean.

_____

_____

_____

_____

1. Write the missing numbers.

4 x _____ = 20	8 x 2 = _____
20 ÷ 4 = _____	16 ÷ 2 = _____
50 ÷ 10 = _____	6 x 5 = _____
5 x _____ = 50	30 ÷ _____ = 6
3 x _____ = 12	10 x 2 = _____
12 ÷ _____ = 4	20 ÷ _____ = 10

2. Divide.

10 ÷ 2 = _____	14 ÷ 2 = _____	18 ÷ 2 = _____
12 ÷ 2 = _____	16 ÷ 8 = _____	30 ÷ 3= _____
6 ÷ 3 = _____	4 ÷2 = _____	20 ÷ 5 = _____
8 ÷ 4 = _____	15 ÷3 = _____	8 ÷ 2 = _____

3. Order the temperatures from highest to lowest.

18° c	- 6° c	12° c

_____, _____, _____

4. What temperature might it be on a really hot summer day? _____

Choose your STRENGTH exercise!

Day 7

Exercise for today:

_____

Check & Record in Fitness Log.

Which One Doesn't Belong?

Read the words. Write the word that doesn't belong on the line. Then tell why the other words belong together.

Ex. **Triangle, circle, pizza, square, rectangle.**   pizza

The other words are shapes.

1. **Basketball, soccer, tennis, boots, golf**_____

_____

2. **Cow, apple, horse, chicken, sheep**_____ _____

_____

3. **Sunday, Friday, March, Monday, Tuesday**_____

_____

4. **Eagle, robin, raccoon, blue jay, hawk** _____

_____

5. **Tulip, daisy, noise, rose, daffodil, lily** _____

_____

6. **Train, house, plane, boat, bike** _____

_____

Read the lists of words above again.

7. **How many one syllable words?** _____

8. **How many two syllable words?** _____

9. **How many three syllable words?** _____

1. Rule is multiply by 10		
Input	I	output
Ex. 5	I	50
4	I	_____
6	I	_____
7	I	_____
9	I	_____

2. Rule is subtract 100		
Input	I	Output
Ex. 654	I	554
897	I	_____
245	I	_____
572	I	_____
932	I	_____

3.Write two multiplication sentences from this array.

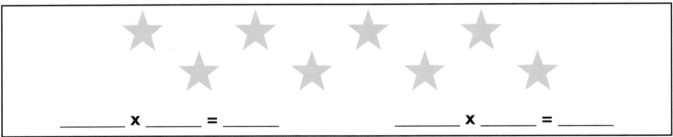

_____ x _____ = _____   _____ x _____ = _____

4.Circle the numbers that are less than 352.

456   153   345   234   322   253

Underline all the even numbers.

5. How much more is the largest number than the smallest number? _____

Choose your **AEROBIC** exercise!

Exercise for today:

_____

Check & Record in Fitness Log.

Day 8

Courtesy and Good Manners

Good manners help us get along with others. Because there are more than 6 billion people on this planet, being courteous is very important.

Unscramble the words then use them to answer the questions.

1. When you ask for something say _____. (lepsea)

2. When someone gives you something say _____ _____. (htnka ouy)

3. When you run into someone say _____ _____. (xecsue em)

4. When you hurt someone or make a mistake you say _____ _____

_____. (I ma osryr)

5. When someone says "thank you" say _____ _____

_____. (oyu rae elwomce)

6. When someone is talking don't _____. (ntirreput)

7. Look up these words in the dictionary and write down the definitions.

etiquette: _____

_____

_____

patience: _____

_____

_____

considerate: _____

_____

_____

1. Congruent shapes are the same size and shape. Circle the congruent shapes in each row.

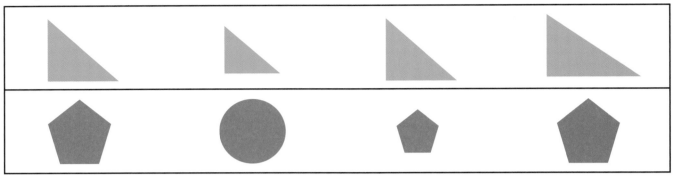

2. Label the colored parts.

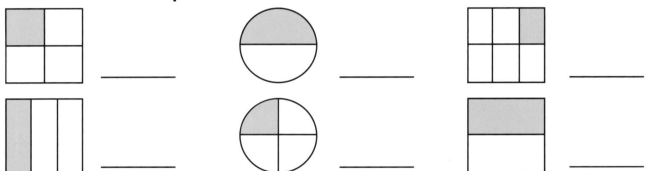

3. Compare the fractions: <, >, =

1/2 _____ 1/4   1/8 _____ 1/4

4. Draw the shapes.

octagon	pentagon	parallelogram	right triangle

Choose your STRENGTH exercise!

Exercise for today:

_____

Check & Record in Fitness Log.

Friendship is spending time with someone else that you care about — animals or people!

Value

KARTICK

Kartick grew up in India near Bannerghatta National Park where he learned to love animals and nature. At night he would go into the park and watch different animals including sloth bears, elephants and leopards drink water from fresh water pools under the moonlight. He showed them respect and did not scare them off by being loud or disruptive. He grew to love the animals very much and cared for their safety. He realized animals were his friends and that he needed to take care of them by protecting the park where they lived. Kartick helped rescue an elephant named Raju from captivity. Raju cried because she was so happy.

True or False

Kartick considers animals to be his friends. _____

During the day Kartick would watch his animal friends play in the fresh water pools. _____

Protecting the environment that animals live is a way to protect and respect our animal friends. _____

Kartick helped rescue an elephant named Raju. _____

Raju cried because she did not want to be rescued. _____

Value:

FRIENDSHIP

"Don't walk behind me; I may not lead. Don't walk in front of me; I may not follow. Just walk beside me and be my friend."

– Winnie the Pooh

```
H O N E S T W S Q M M H B E T O H L
P K K P K H U C V C Z S E R U D R U
G D X D O O C P P B H N U F E M S F
W A K W R Y R F I A G D V A Z D Q T
F U V E L O P D N J I V C A O S Y C
E G N M K L Y U O K L P E K W J R E
Y E L K K L I E H H O Q H H O O T P
G I J I K T D S U T Y Z Z C T M W S
E K N B A P Y K T J A M R D O Z B E
N D C U W T P X U E L L P W B G K R
Z R Y B W L M B K S N N R Q Z D B H
X R G G U F Q J S R P P S T K I M V
G W V C U K B D R Z W N N V G T A B
U P G J G K L D G X U T H B R I C I
Y I A F Q S X S U I B P R L L H E P
K N I P F B J Y D M R K U O J T Q P
```

Find the words below that are qualities of a good friend.

WORD BANK

fun	listen
loyal	generous
honest	respectful
kind	

Be a Good Friend

 Invite a friend over. Let them choose what to play first.

 Watch *Toy Story* with your family. Talk about how the characters in the movie portray true friendship.

 Make a friendship bracelet for one of your friends. Give it to them and tell them why you are happy to be friends.

 **Day 10**

Choose a **Play** or **Exercise** Activity!

124

2-3 • © Summer Fit Activities"

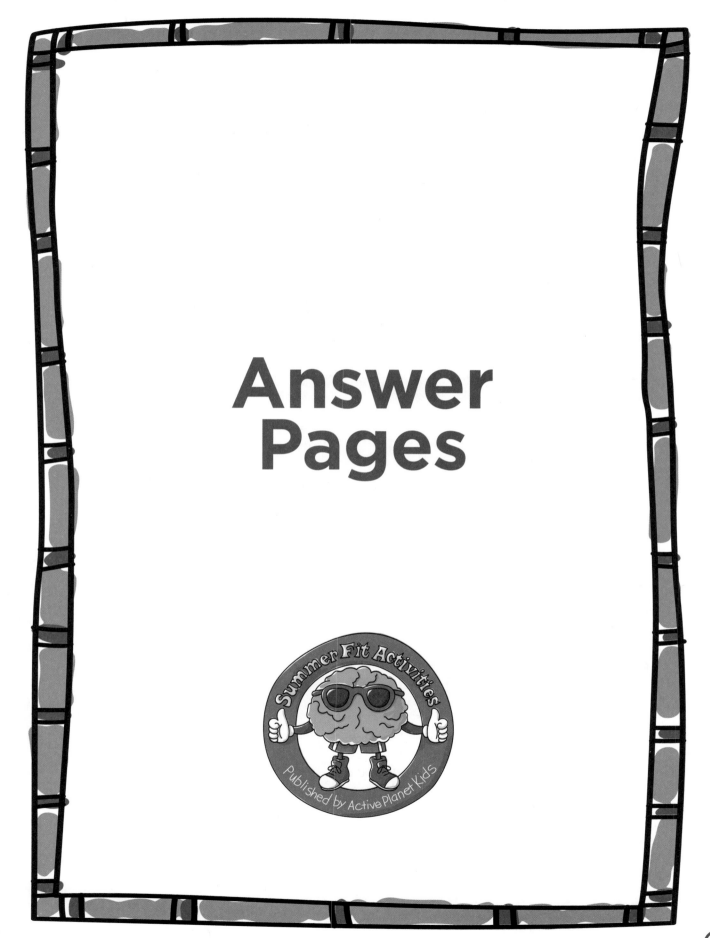

Answer
Pages

Summer Fit Activities
Published by Active Planet Kids

Answer Key

P. 1-4
Summer Skills Review Reading

1. a. ran, jumped b. kicked
2. a. Jason, Garret, father, car
   b. hose, towels
3. home, work
4. birdhouse
5. a. ! b. ? c. .
6. a. her b. his
7. a. home work
   b. chick en
   c. basket ball
8. a. cats b. foxes c. babies
9. a. large b. see c. silent
   (answers may vary)
10. a. quiet b. whisper c. slow
    (answers may vary)
11. a. I'll   b. they'll
    c. he's   d. we're
    e. let's   f. she's
12. a. slimy b. scary
    c. stinky (answers may vary)
13. bathtub, below, brain, bucket
14. hottest

Summer Skills Review Math
1. a. 10 b. 19 c. 2 d. 10 e. 14 f. 7
2. 14, 140, 80, 16, 8
3. a. < b. > c. = d. > e. = f. <
4. X, X ,O
5. 13
6. 6, 8, 10, 12, 14, 16, 18
7. 30, 40, 50, 60, 70, 80, 90
8. 2, 5, 7, 9
9. 3, 4, 8, 7, 6
10. 3, 6, 1, 4, 2
11. (line drawn through
    middle of each shape)
12. a. 54 b. 12 c. 23 d. 2
13. a. 6:15 b. 9:30 c. 12:10 d. 2:45
14. 10 - 7 = 3
15. a. hexagon drawn
    b. triangle drawn
    c. rectangle drawn
    d. square drawn.

p. 7:
big/large, grin/smile, look/see, little/small, shout/yell, happy/glad, quick/fast, sad/unhappy, jump/leap, intelligent/smart

1. quiet   2. pretty   3. hard

p. 8:
1. one hundred fifty
2. three hundred twenty-five
3. four hundred eighteen
4. eight hundred sixty-three.
5. 652   6. 319   7. 875   8. 127

p. 9:
1. True   2. false   3. false
4. true   5. false
6. less, smallest
7. least, few
8. bad, nothing

p. 10:
1. 8 + 2 = 10, 2 + 8 = 10,
   10 – 8 = 2, 10 – 2 = 8
2. 5 + 8 = 13, 8 + 5 = 13,
   13 – 8 = 5, 13 – 5 = 8
3. 4, 6, 8, 10, 12, 14, 16, 18.
4. 6, 9, 12, 15, 18, 21, 24, 27.
5. 8, 12, 16, 20, 24, 28, 32, 36
6. 10, 15, 20, 25, 30, 35, 40, 45.

p. 11:
1. beaches 2. foxes
3. peaches 4. books
5. houses 6. dogs
7. boys   8. hens
9. boxes   10. dresses
11. children 12. men
13. women 14. teeth
15. babies 16. ladies
17. cries   18. flies

p. 12:
1. 114, 142, 156, 188, 190
2. 223, 246, 287, 295, 305
3. 500, 504, 515, 550, 555
4. $1.03   5. $1.60   6. $1.31

p. 13:
1. shoe, shark
2. sun, owl.
3. zoo, smile, rocket.
4. ant, corn, house.
5. answers vary
6. campfire, marshmallows
7. children, bridge, water.
8. bird, branch, tree.
9. sister, zoo, animals.

p. 14:
1. cups
2. feet.
3. 3:45 on clock.
4. 1:00
5. 8:15 and quarter past 8.
6. July. November.

p. 15:
1. dishonest
2. after
3. lie
4. everything
5. never
6. worst.

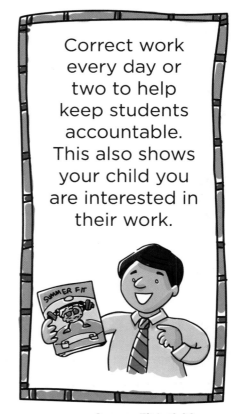

Correct work every day or two to help keep students accountable. This also shows your child you are interested in their work.

Answer Key

p. 19:
1. Mr.   2. Sat.
3. Dr.   4. Ave.
5. lbs.   6. Oct.
7. Mon. Tues. Wed.
   Thurs. Fri. Sat.

p. 20:
1. 10   2. 16
3. 15   4. 12
5. 2,6,8,10,12,14,16,18,20,22

p. 21:
eggs, tadpole, frogs
1. amphibians
2. tadpoles
3. places
4. webbed
5. insects

p. 22:
1. 4   2. 6   3. 4
4. 10   5. $1.20   6. $1.00

p. 23:
1. daisy, rose, sunflower, tulip.
2. shark, sting ray, dolphin,
   swordfish
3. elephant, zebra, monkey, lion.
4. shoes, hat, coat, socks.
5. Arizona, Utah,
   Michigan, Alaska.
6-8. Answers Vary

p. 24:
1. 124, 126 ; 88;90, 110; 112,
   344;346, 199;201, 66;68.
2. centimeters, inches, feet,
   gallon, quart, ounce.
3. 3,6,9,12,15,18,21,24,27,30.

p. 25:
1. bear   2. bare   3. know
4. no   5. pear   6. pair
7. sun   8. son   9. sea
10. see   11. for, four

p. 26:
shapes colored as directed,
lines of symmetry through
each shape.

p. 27:
I help those in need.
I think about how my actions
affect others.
I apologize when I hurt
someone.

p. 31:
1. 4 parts   2. slipping
3. helmet   4. exercise

p. 32:
1. >,<,<,<,=, >
2. <,=,=,<,<,>,=
3. A,B, B,A, B,B
4. moon, star, sun, moon, star;
   triangle, circle, square,
   square, triangle

p. 33:
1. he's   2. didn't   3. won't
4. they've   5. wasn't   6. she's
7. can't   8. he'll   9. we're
10. we'll   11. it's
12. they're.
I'll/I will, shouldn't/should not,
doesn't/does not,
you're/you are,
hasn't/has not, that's/that is.

p. 34:
1. 7, 6, 8, 9, 5, 7, 6,
   60, 9, 18, 400, 50
2. 10, 20, 30, 40, 50,
   60, 70, 80, 90, 100.
3. 74 cents

p. 35:
dragonfly, swordfish, pancake,
skateboard, birdhouse, football,
sunshine, popcorn
1-4. answers vary.

p. 36:
1. 500 + 60 + 3
2. 900 + 10 + 6
3. 4,000 + 300 + 80 + 3
4. 800 + 70 + 5
5. 1,000 + 600 + 20 + 4
6. 6,000 + 900 + 50 + 7
7. 264   8. 189   9. 513
10. 1,648   11. 3,263   12. 9, 420

p. 37:
fist, rib cage, blood,
four, pulse, faster

p. 38:
1. 16 inches
2. 20 inches
3. 16 inches
4. 9 inches
5. 10 feet

p. 39:
1. true   2. false
3. true   4. true

Reward well
done and
completed work
with stickers,
stamps or
hand written
messages.

2-3 • © Summer Fit Activities™

Answer Key

p. 43:
1-6. answers vary
7. older, shiny, new, red.
8. cool, blue, hot, summer.

p. 44:
1. 50, 90, 50, 30, 40, 10, 80, 60, 90
2. 70, 70, 40, 80. 3. 53, 80, 86,
   65, 715, 244, 280, 550

p. 45:
1. puppy   2. out
3. hear   4. fly
5. vegetable
6. man.

p. 46:
1. 19.   2. 15.   3. 38.
4. 46.   5. 49.   6. 97.
7. 4 tens 8 ones
8. 6 tens 3 ones
9. 9 tens 8 ones
10. 7 tens 5 ones
11. 76   12. 89.
13. 18   14. 33

Use a timer to motivate your child to stay on task and finish their work in a timely manner.

p. 47:
ai, ee, oa, ea, ai, oa,
oa, oo, ee, oo, ee, ai

p. 48:
1. soccer   2. football
3. 4   4. tennis, volleyball
5. 3:30   6. 1:20
7. 8:55   8. 11:10
9. 12:45

p. 49:
1. ?   2. .
3. .   4. !!
5. ?   6. .
7-8. answers vary.

p. 50:
1. pentagon, 5, 5
2. octagon, 8, 8
3. yes, no.

p. 51:
1. focus, dedication, diligence.
Answers vary.

p. 55: Answers vary

p. 56:
1. 17, 60, 58, 56, 22, 326, 972,
   489, 561, 703
2. Answers vary

p. 57:
1. pets: 4,3,1,2,5
2. fruit: 5,4,2,1,3.
3. body parts: 2,3,4,1,5.
4. colors: 5,2,1,3,4.
5. sealife: 2,4,5,1,3.

p. 58:
1. $16.25   2. $35.85
3. $8.05   4. $57.30
5. answers vary
6. $2.00

p. 59:
1. 7   2. North America
3. 5   4. Pacific
5. through the center.

p. 60:
1. $6.25   2. $3.75
3. chicken fingers   4. coffee

p. 61:
1. date   2. greeting
3. body   4. closing
5. signature

p. 62:
1. 8 in.   2. 4 in.
3. 11 in.   4. 9 square units.
5. 6 square units
6. 100   7. 3

p. 63: Answers vary

p 67:
1. song's   2. Sam's
3. bird's   4. teacher's
5. boy's   6. parents'
7. snake's   8. mom's
9. singers' 10. king's

p. 68:
1. 25,45; 50, 70;
   10, 30; 35, 55; 90, 110
2. 3 tens 5 ones, 9 tens, 8 ones,
   4 tens 4 ones, 7 tens 5 ones,
   1 ten 1 one, 5 tens four ones.
3. 75, 33, 92, 41

p. 69:
top to bottom:
2,3,2,3,3,3,1,2,1,2,3,1,2.

p. 70:
1. 632   2. 571   3. 965
4. 390   5. 104   6. 500
7. 600   8. 400   9. 800
10. 300   11. 300   12. =
13. >   14. >   15. >

2-3 • © Summer Fit Activities™

Answer Key

p. 71:
1. aphids   2. 3,6
3. spots   4. winter   5. bad

p. 72:
1. 2,4,6,8,10   2. 30
3. 1,3,5,7,9   4. 25
5. 8 + 3 + 4 =15
6. 10   7. 7   8. 2

p. 73:
1. ant   2. Aunt   3. week
4. weak   5. write   6. right
7. ate   8. eight   9. wear
10. where   11. pear   12. pair

p. 74:
1. 7 sq. units
2. 5 sq. units
3. flip   4. turn

p. 75: Answers vary

p. 79:
1. her   2. he   3. they
4. we   5. it   6. us
7. she   8. them

p. 80:
1. 627   2. 869
3. 469   4. 469, 627, 869

p. 81:
1. L   2. S   3. G
4. G   5. L   6. S
7. G   8. S   9. G
10. S   11. L   12. L

p. 82:
Gray spiders:
58, 24, 56, 84, 2
Brown spiders:
23, 11, 17, 25, 23,
Pattern:
6,9,12,15,18, 21,
24, 27, 30, 33,
Circled numbers:
6,12,18,24,30,36

p. 83:
(left to right) st,tr, bl, pl, st, fr, fl,
br, cl, sh, dr, tr, sp, sl, cr, ch, sn,
gl, sp, ch, sh, th, fl, pl.

p. 84:
12,6,0,18,21,30,27,24,15,33. 6

p. 85:
13, Dear Alex, We; June 10th,
Would; us? We're; s'mores.
Please; know; come. ; It; fun!
Your Friend,
Josh.

p. 86:
1. 2   2. 20   3. 4
4. 13   5. 65

p. 87:
justice/fairness, harmony/
peace, respect/admiration,
independence/freedom

p. 91:
1. I rode my bike to Sunset Park.
2. We saw monkeys at the zoo.
3. I have soccer practice on
   Wednesday.
4. My sister and I made cookies
   for Grandma.
5. Do you like to collect stamps?
6. The flowers we planted in the
   spring are blooming now.

p. 92: Answers vary.
8,12,16,20,24,28,32,36. 4

p. 93:
1. robin   2. a nest
3. cherry   4. eggs
5. keep   6. out
7. nest with baby birds
8. shan't, I'm, don't, I'll.

p. 94:
1. 11 cm.   2. 3 cm.
3. 2 in.   4. 4 in.

p. 95:
1. lk,   2. nk
3. st   4. nt
5. nd   6. mp
7. lf   8. lt
9. wh   10. sch
11. th   12. gn
13. th   14. gh
15. ck   16. sh
17. ph   18. wr
19. kn   20. kn
21. th   22. ch
23. th   24. ch
25. th   26. wr
27. sh   28. th
29. ch   30. ck
31. gh   32. ph

p. 96:
1. 9x2 = 18   2. 4x3 = 12
3. 4 x 10 = 40
4. $3.02, $.98   5. 3:45

Have your child correct their own work while you read off the answers. This will reinforce the skills they just practiced.

Answer Key

p. 97:
1. taste buds   2. brain
3. salty, sweet, sour, bitter.
4. sweet.   5. sour
6-8. answers vary.

p. 98:
1. 36   2. 1   3. 60
4. 1   5. 24   6. 1
7. measurements as directed.
8. 8,9,6,5; 4,6,4,0; 9,0,2,7; 5,9,3,2.

p. 99:
hard/difficult; began started;
raised/earned; called/named

p. 103:
1. ch. 6   2. ch. 9
3. p. 11   4. a healthy body
5. ch. 7   6. pgs. 17-19

p. 104:
1. 6, 8, 10, 14, 2; 24, 12, 6, 15, 3;
    0, 5, 20, 30, 25; 16, 8, 0, 4, 12;
    60, 40, 10, 80, 20.
2. 600, 100, 300, 800, 600, 300,
    200, 900, 500

Give your student an opportunity to rework missed questions. Go over any mistakes made together.

p. 105:
Long i: cry, sky, why,shy,try,
     fly,reply.
Long e: family, library, sunny,
     puppy, lady, baby,
     penny.
1. library   2. family
3. baby   4. sunny
5. fly

p. 106:
1. 5   2. July 24th
3. Thursday
4. July 27th
5. 4   6. Wednesday
7. Jan. Feb. Mar. April,
    May, June, July, Aug.
    Sept. Oct. Nov. Dec.

p. 107:
Forest =(pine tree, deer.
Desert =(cactus,snake,sun.
Pond =(water,reeds,frog.

p. 108:
715, 998, 877

p. 109:
1. 3,4,2,5,1   2. 5,3,2,1,4

p. 110:
1. line
2. ray
3. line segment
angles a,c,f circled.

p. 111:
definitions from dictionary.

p. 115:
1. proper nouns:
    Albert Einstein, Pizza Palace,
    Tom's, Mary, Evergreen Library,
    Yellowstone Park, June,
    Grand Canyon, Arizona.
    Common nouns:
    physicist, brother,
    birthday, friend.
2. answer vary

p. 116:
1. 16, 15, 8, 6, 6, 0, 20,
    8, 4, 12, 18, 1 2, 4, 0, 9
2. 20   3. 20   4. 17
5. 0   6. 8

p. 117: Answers vary.

p. 118:
1. 5,5; 5,10; 4,3; 16,8; 30,5; 20
2. 2. 5,6,2,2,7,2,2,5,9,10,4,4
3. 18,12,-6   4. 100 degrees

p. 119:
1. boots; sport
2. apple; farm animals
3. March; days of the week.
4. raccoon; birds
5. noise; flowers
6. house; transportation.
7. 14   8. 14   9. 2

p. 120:
1. 40, 60, 70, 90.
2. 797, 145, 472, 832
3. 4 x 2 = 8, 2 x 4 = 8
4. 153, 345, 234, 322, 253.
    Underlined: 456, 234, 322.
5. 303.

p. 121:
1. please   2. thank you
3. excuse me   4. I am sorry
5. you are welcome   6. interrupt
7. definitions from dictionary.

p. 122:
1. first and third triangle,
    first and fourth pentagon.
2. 1/4, 1/2, 1/6, 1/3, 1/4, 1/2
3. >, <
4. octagon. pentagon.
    parallelogram. right triangle.

p. 123:
1. T   2. F   3. T
4. T   5. F

Summer Fit Book Report I

Title: _____

Author: _____

Illustrator: _____

Setting (Where the story takes place): _____

Main Character(s):

_____

_____

_____

Write your favorite part of the story
(use separate sheet of paper if needed):

_____

_____

_____

_____

_____

_____

_____

_____

_____

_____

_____

Tell your favorite part of the story to a parent, guardian or friend.

Read a variety of books on topics that interest you already and new areas that you want to explore!

Summer Fit Book Report II

Title: _____

Author: _____

Illustrator: _____

Setting (Where the story takes place): _____

Main Character(s):

_____

_____

_____

Write your favorite part of the story
(use separate sheet of paper if needed):

_____

_____

_____

_____

_____

_____

_____

_____

_____

_____

Tell your favorite part of the story to a parent, guardian or friend.

Read a variety of books on topics that interest you already and new areas that you want to explore!

Summer Fit Book Report III

Title: _____

Author: _____

Illustrator: _____

Setting (Where the story takes place): _____

Main Character(s):

_____

_____

_____

Write your favorite part of the story
(use separate sheet of paper if needed):

_____

_____

_____

_____

_____

_____

_____

_____

_____

_____

_____

Tell your favorite part of the story to a parent, guardian or friend.

Read a variety of books on topics that interest you already and new areas that you want to explore!

Summer Fit Book Report IV

Title: _____

Author: _____

Illustrator: _____

Setting (Where the story takes place): _____

Main Character(s):

_____

_____

_____

Write your favorite part of the story
(use separate sheet of paper if needed):

_____

_____

_____

_____

_____

_____

_____

_____

_____

Tell your favorite part of the story to a parent, guardian or friend.

Read a variety of books on topics that interest you already and new areas that you want to explore!

HEALTH
&
NUTRITION

Let's Play

There are so many ways to play! Check off the different activities as you play them, have fun!

Everybody has different abilities and interests, so take the time to figure out what activities and exercises you like. Try them all: soccer, dance, karate, basketball and skating are only a few. After you have played a lot of different ones, go back and focus on the ones you like! Create your own ways to be active and combine different activities and sports to put your own twist on things. Talk with your parents or caregiver for ideas and have them help you find and do the activities that you like best. Playing and exercising is a great way to help you become fit, but remember that the most important thing about playing is that you are having fun!

List of Exercise Activities

Home–Outdoor:

Walking
Ride Bicycle
Swimming
Walk Dog
Golf with whiffle balls outside
Neighborhood walks/Exploring (in a safe area)
Hula Hooping
Rollerskating/Rollerblading
Skateboarding
Jump rope
Climbing trees
Play in the back yard
Hopscotch
Stretching
Basketball
Yard work
Housecleaning

Home – Indoor:

Dancing
Exercise DVD
Yoga DVD
Home gym equipment
Stretch bands
Free weights
Stretching

With friends or family:

Red Rover
Chinese jump rope
Regular jump rope
Ring around the rosie
Tag/Freeze
Four score
Capture the flag
Dodgeball
Slip n Slide
Wallball
Tug of War
Stretching
Run through a sprinkler
Skipping
Family swim time
Bowling
Basketball
Hiking
Red light, Green light
Kick ball
Four Square
Tennis
Frisbee
Soccer
Jump Rope
Baseball

Turn off TV Go Outside - PLAY!
Public Service Announcement Brought to you by Summer Fit

Chill out on Screen Time

Screen time is the amount of time spent watching TV, DVDs or going to the movies, playing video games, texting on the phone and using the computer. The more time you spend looking at a screen the less time you are outside riding your bike, walking, swimming or playing soccer with your friends. Try to spend no more than a couple hours a day in front of a screen for activities other than homework and get outside and play!

2-3 • © Summer Fit Activities™

HEALTHY BODIES

There are many ways to enrich your life by eating healthy, exercising each day and playing! Keeping your body strong and healthy will help you feel good and even perform better in school. To be healthy, you need to eat right, get enough sleep and exercise. What you learn and do with Summer Fit Activities™ is just the beginning. From here, you will be able to find other healthy and active things to do based on your interests, abilities and personal goals.

 Aerobic Exercises help your cardiovascular system that includes your heart and blood vessels. You need a strong heart to pump blood. Your blood delivers oxygen and nutrients to your body.

 Strength Exercises help you make your muscles stronger and increase your muscular endurance. Endurance helps you get the most from your muscles before you get tired!!

 Flexibility Exercises are good for many reasons including warming up before you do aerobic or strength exercises. Flexibility also helps you use all your muscles in different ways, positions and ranges of motion.

Your body composition is made up of lean mass and fat mass. Lean mass includes water, muscles and organs in your body. Fat mass includes fat your body needs for later and stores for energy.

Exercise helps you burn body fat and do more of the activities you want to do like hiking, biking and playing at the beach. There are a lot fun sports and activities to choose from that will help you strengthen your body and your brain!

Get Active!

Apple	Brain
Water	Vegetable
Exercise	Muscles
Aerobic	Organs
Strength	Fun
Flexibility	Play

```
D G L H B J S Z V Z B R F P C
Y H V T T E V E V A Z Y L F I
A C U P L G G M Y K I V E S B
G O T C A E N G H T P W X M O
H E S X T L M E Y A L P I L R
A U Y A E S I C R E X E B V E
M P B Y B M R G B T H Z I Q A
I L P R O L S V V F S R L K X
E Y A L D P E N B G A R I I I
F I B P E L H Y U V I F T W N
N G T D J A U D L F Z Q Y A X
O N M C X A V R S I V J S T J
O R G A N S B W A K K R A E C
J T C E L Y R C U Z R B G R P
X J P Y A W W E O S C K I K J
```

Active Lifestyle Pop Quiz!

What does being active mean to you?

List your 3 favorite aerobic activities

1) _____

2) _____

3) _____

EX: *bicycling, running, swimming, skateboarding, hiking*

List 2 sports you like to play

1) _____

2) _____

EX: *lacrosse, basketball, baseball, dance, volleyball*

List 3 activities you like that help build strength and flexibility

1) _____

2) _____

3) _____

EX: *yoga, dance, gymnastics, martial arts, jump rope*

List 3 fun things you like to do that get you moving

1) _____

2) _____

3) _____

EX: *bowling, skating, fishing, gardening, cooking*

List 2 things you can limit that will help you be more active:

1) _____

2) _____

EX: *video games, T.V, phone*

List 3 things you can do to help the environment and get you moving more often!

1) _____

2) _____

3) _____

EX: *pick up trash in neighborhood, separate items in recycling bins, help plant a garden, wash your water cup and reuse, ride your bike*

2–3 • © Summer Fit Activities™

Summer Fitness Program

The goal of your Summer Fitness program is to help you improve in all areas of physical fitness and to be active every day.

You build cardiovascular endurance through aerobic exercise. For aerobic exercise, you need to work large muscle groups that get your heart pumping and oxygen moving through your entire body. This increases your heart rate and breathing. On your aerobic day, you can jog, swim, hike, dance, skateboard, ride your bike, roller blade... there are so many to choose from

Your goal should be to try to get 30 minutes a day of aerobic exercise at least 2-3 times a week. Follow your daily Summer Fit™ exercise schedule and choose your own aerobic exercises along the way.

You build your muscular strength and muscle endurance with exercises that work your muscles, like push-ups, sit-ups and pull-ups. Increase how many you can do of each of these over time and pay attention to your Summer Fit ™daily exercises for other activities that help build strong muscles.

Get loose – stretch. Warming up before you exercise if very important. It prepares your body for exercising by loosening your muscles and getting your body ready for training. An easy start is to shake your arms and roll your shoulders!

Time to Hydrate

It is important to drink water before and after you exercise because water regulates your body temperature and gives you nutrients to keep you healthy.

The next time you exercise, drink a cup of water before and after you are done.

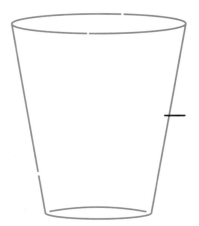

Color the bottom half of the cup red below to represent the water you drink before you exercise. Color the top half of the cup blue to represent the water you drink after you exercise.

Water Facts

There is the same amount of water on earth today as there was when dinosaurs roamed through our backyards!

75% of your brain is water!

Water regulates the earth's temperature.

Water is made up of two elements, hydrogen and oxygen. Its chemical formula is H2O

Water is essential for life on earth.

Here are instructions for your daily exercises. Talk with a parent about setting goals. Set your goals for time or reps. Keep track of your goals using your Summer Fitness Chart. Have fun!

Aerobic Exercises and Activities

Tag: Decide who is "IT." Choose the boundaries for the game. If a player crosses the boundaries, during the game he/she is automatically "IT."

Give players a 15 second head start. "IT" counts to 15 and then chases the others to tag them! The player who has been tagged is now "IT!"

Foot Bag: Everybody who wants to play gathers in a circle about four or five feet across. Serve the foot bag by tossing it gently, about waist high. Keep the foot bag in the air using any part of your body except arms or hands. Pass the foot bag back and forth around the circle as long as possible without it touching the ground.

Tree Sprints: Use two trees that are 10-15 feet apart. Start with your left leg touching the base of the tree. On "Go" sprint as fast as you can to the opposite tree, touch the tree trunk, and sprint back to your start position. Continue sprints until you complete your goal or get tired.

Jumping Jacks: Stand with your back straight and knees crouched down a little. Place your arms at your side. Jump in place, raising your hands above your head and clapping while moving your feet apart. Count each time you clap your hands. Continue until you reach your goal or get tired.

Cross-Country Skier: Start in a medium crouch position with one leg in front of the other. Lean forward slightly, keep your knees flexed and bounce in place switching your front foot with your rear foot while swinging your arms back and forth with each bounce. Count 1 rep for each time you reach your start position. Continue until you reach your goal or get tired.

Hide and Seek: Select an area to play. Designate a specific area with clear boundaries. Have everyone gather around a tree or other landmark, which is "home base." Whoever goes first must close his/her eyes and count to 10. Everybody else hides during the count. After the count is over, call out "Ready or not here I come!" Now it's time to look for the other players who are hiding. They are trying to get to home base before they are found. If they get to home base without being found they are "safe." The first player found loses and they start the next game by counting to 10!

Turtle and Rabbit: This is a running exercise that you do by running in place. Start in turtle mode by running 25 steps in place very slowly. Then, be a rabbit and run 25 steps as fast as you can!

Wheel Over: Lie down on your back. Raise your legs off the ground and pretend you are riding your bike in the air. Try to keep your back flat on the floor or ground.

Run or Jog: Jog or run in your backyard or neighborhood. Pump your arms, keep your back straight, flex your knees, and stay on your toes. Continue for as long as you can or until you reach your time goal.

Toss and Run (bean bag): Find a start place in your backyard or neighborhood park. Toss your beanbag in front of you 5 feet. Walk to pick it up. Toss your beanbag 10 feet. Jog to pick it up. Toss your beanbag 15 feet. Run as fast as you can to pick it up! Repeat as many times as needed to complete your goal. If space is limited, toss back and forth to the same place.

Freeze Tag: In Freeze Tag, everybody tries to stay away from whomever is "It." When you are tagged, you "freeze" in your tracks until somebody unfreezes you by crawling between your legs without being tagged themselves. When somebody is tagged for the third time, he/she is "It!"

Egg Race (spoon and egg): Mark a start and finish line 10-15 feet away. Balance an egg on a spoon and race to the finish line! Whomever crosses first wins, but be careful, if you drop your egg you lose!

Scissor Swim: Lie down on your stomach. Raise your legs 6-8 inches up and down like scissors. Pretend you are cutting the water like a huge pair of scissors! Keep your legs straight and your stomach flat on the ground.

Stepping on Up: Climb the stairs in your house or apartment. Raise your legs high on each step. Climb slow and steady. Set a goal on how many steps you can climb.

Hill Run (Jog): Find a hill at a park or neighborhood. Run (or jog) up the hill. Pump your arms, keep your back straight, flex your knees, and stay on your toes. Set a goal on how many times you can run (or jog) the hill.

Hi Yah!: Stand with both your feet planted on the ground. When you are ready, kick the air with one leg and scream, "Hi-Yah!" When your foot is planted, kick your other leg, "Hi-Yah!" Go slow and set a goal on how many times you can kick without losing your balance.

Wild: Find an area in your backyard or park. Run, scream, wave your hands in the air, jump up and down, roll on the grass – have fun!

Strength Exercises and Activities

Ankle Touches: Lie with your back on the ground. Bend your knees up with your feet flat on the ground. Alternate from left to right touching left hand to left heel and right hand to right heel.

Push-ups: Lie chest-down with your hands at shoulder level, palms flat on the floor, and feet together. Let yourself down slowly as far as you can go. Straighten your arms and push your body up off the floor. Try not to bend as you push up. Pause for a moment before you do another. Set a goal on how many you can do in a row.

Moon Touches: Stand with both feet together and back straight. Bend your knees and both arms in front of your body. Jump straight up with both feet and reach up as you jump with your left and then your right arm. Set a goal on how many you can do without stopping.

Sky Reach: Choose a small object such as a ball, a book or even a piece of fruit. Make an "L" with your arm—with your upper arm at shoulder level and your forearm pointing toward the ceiling. Now extend your arm straight over your shoulder, pushing the object toward the sky. Return to your starting position.

Fly in the Ointment: Stand straight with your arms stretched out and opened wide. Keep your back straight and bend your knees just a little bit. Slowly touch one knee to the floor while clapping your hands. Return to starting position and start over by touching the opposite knee to the floor and clapping.

Jump Rope: Start by holding an end of the rope in each hand. Position the rope behind you on the ground. Raise your arms up and turn the rope over your head bringing it down in front of you. When it reaches the ground, jump over it. Find a good pace, not too slow and not too fast. Jump over the rope each time it comes around. Continue until you reach your goal of jumping a certain amount of times without stopping.

Bear Crawl: Crouch down on your hands and feet. Slowly move forward stretching your arms out as far as you can in front of you. Stay low on all fours and growl like a bear! How many times can you go around your yard on all fours?

Hula-Hoop: Hold the hula-hoop around your waist with both hands. Pull it forward so it is resting against your back. With both hands, fling the hoop to the left so that rolls in a circle around your body. Do this a few times until you get the feel of it. Leave the hula-hoop on the ground for a few minutes and practice swirling your hip. Move your pelvis left, back, right, forward. Find a groove and keep the hoop going around your hips as long as you can. When it falls to the ground pick it up and try again!

Crab Crawl: Sit on the ground with your arms behind you and your legs in front. Move your legs forward followed by your arms. Watch out for sand traps!

Modified Push Up: Get in your push-up position and then rest on your knees on the ground. When you are ready to start, lower your body straight down while rocking forward on your knees to help take away some of your body weight. Push back up so you are in your original position. This is a great way to start learning push-ups and building your strength.

Freeze Dance: Play this with your friends! Put on your favorite music and dance! When the music stops, everybody freezes!

Bottle curls: Start with two bottles of laundry detergent (or any large bottle with a handle). Stand with your feet flat on the floor, shoulder width apart. Place both your hands in the same position on the handles of each bottle. With your back straight, slowly curl each bottle keeping your arm in the shape of an "L" until the bottle is raised to your shoulder. Only use bottles that you can lift easily and that do not cause you to stumble under their weight.

Snake Curl: Lie on your back with knees bent, feet flat on the ground, and a beanbag between your knees to keep them together. Lay your hands on your side. Curl up and lay back in your starting position. Repeat!

Chair Leg-lifts: Put a small chair next to you. Standing next to the chair, rest one hand lightly on the back (the back of the chair is facing you). Slowly lift one leg with your knee bent. Now, slowly lower your leg until your foot almost touches the ground. How many can you do?

Giraffe Walk: Stand up tall with your feet firmly planted on the floor. Keep your back straight and upright. Reach your arms over your head and skip forward twice. Then, slowly walk forward twice again and do another skip.

Can Do: Go to the kitchen and find two of the heaviest cans you can hold. Stand with your feet flat on the floor, with the cans in your hands and arms at your side. Lift the cans up to your chest, bending your arms at the elbows. Hold for two seconds, and then slowly lower your arms.

Bottle Lift: Start with two bottles of laundry detergent (or any large bottle with a handle). Stand with your feet flat on the floor, shoulder width apart. Place the bottles on each side of your feet. Bend your knees, grab the bottles and stand up.

Bunny Bounce: Stand with feet together, knees slightly bent and hands touching your ears. Hop first on your right foot and then on your left. Now, jump with both feet spread apart and then continue hopping, first on the right, then on the left foot!

Crab Kick: Get down in a crab position with your body supported with your hands and feet, and your back towards the ground. Keep your seat up and let your body sag. Kick your right leg in the air. After you have done this 5-10 times switch to your left and repeat.

Gorilla Walk: Spread your feet apart as wide as your shoulders. Bend at your waist and grab your ankles. Hold your ankles and walk stiff legged.

Milk Bottle Lifts: Clean and rinse out 2 quart plastic milk bottles. Fill them with water and screw the caps on tight. Slowly lift them up over your head by extending your arm straight up. Once you do the right, return to starting position. Extend your left arm and repeat. Alternate between arms.

2-3 • © Summer Fit Activities"

NUTRITION

Hey Parents!

A healthy diet and daily exercise will maximize the likelihood of your child growing up healthy and strong. Children are constantly growing and adding bone and muscle mass, so a balanced diet is very important to their overall health. Try to provide three nutritious meals a day that all include fruits and vegetables. Try to limit fast food and cook at home as often as you can. Not only is it better on your pocketbook, cooking at home is better for you and can be done together as a family. Everyone can help and it is more likely you will eat together as a family.

As a healthy eating goal, avoid food and drinks that are high in sugar as much as possible. Provide fresh fruits, vegetables, grains, lean meats, chicken, fish and low-fat dairy items as much as possible.

---

5 Steps to Improve Eating Habits

 Make fresh fruits and vegetables readily available

 Cook more at home, and sit down for dinner as a family.

 Limit sugary drinks, cereals and desserts

 Serve smaller portions

 Limit snacks to 1 or 2 daily

2-3 • © Summer Fit Activities™

HEALTHY EATING POP QUIZ!

What does eating healthy mean to <u>you</u>?

List your 3 favorite healthy foods:

1) _____   2) _____   3) _____

If you were only to eat vegetables,
what 5 vegetables would you choose?

1) _____   2) _____

3) _____   4) _____   5) _____

Fill in the names of 5 different food groups on the Food Plate.

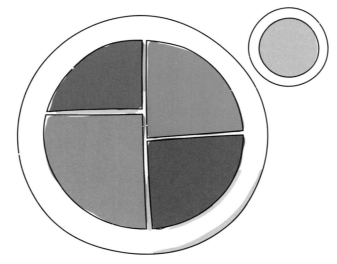

Circle the food and drink items that are healthy foods from the list below:

Milk	Apple	Chicken	Salad
candy	butter	soda	orange
ice cream	carrot	cotton candy	chocolate shake

List your 3 favorite healthy foods

1) _____   2) _____   3) _____

Create a list of foods you would like to grow in a garden

2-3 • © Summer Fit Activities™

Nutrition – *Food Plate*

It is important to eat different foods from the 5 different food groups. Eating a variety of foods helps you stay healthy. Some foods give you protein and fats. Other foods give you vitamins, minerals and carbohydrates. Your body needs all of these to grow healthy and strong!

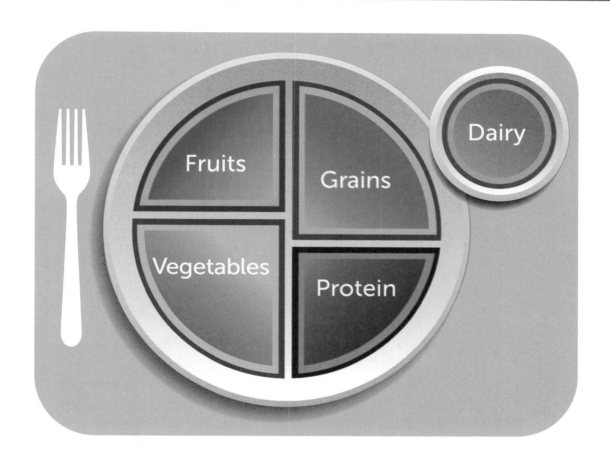

List 3 different foods for each category.

Fruits	Vegetables	Grains	Protein	Dairy
1) _____	1) _____	1) _____	1) _____	1) _____
2) _____	2) _____	2) _____	2) _____	2) _____
3) _____	3) _____	3) _____	3) _____	3) _____

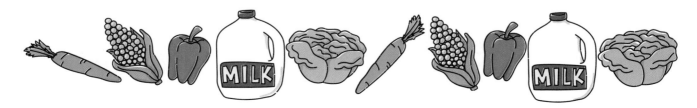

Nutrition – *Meal Planner*

Plan out 3 balanced meals for one day.
Organize your meals so you will eat all the
recommended foods listed on the Food Plate.

BREAKFAST

LUNCH

DINNER

2-3 • © Summer Fit Activities™

Nutrition – *Meal Tracker*

Use these charts to list the different foods from the different
food categories on My Plate that you eat each day.
Every day you mark each food category color in the vegetable!

	Grains	Dairy	Protein	Fruits	Vegetables	
Monday						
Tuesday						
Wednesday						
Thursday						
Friday						
Saturday						
Sunday						

	Grains	Dairy	Protein	Fruits	Vegetables	
Monday						
Tuesday						
Wednesday						
Thursday						
Friday						
Saturday						
Sunday						

MY OWN HEALTHY SNACKS

Frozen Banana Slices

Prep Time: 10 minutes

Freezer Time: 2 hours

Yield: 2 servings, Good for all ages!

Ingredients: 2 fresh bananas

Directions: Peel the bananas and cut them into 5-6 slices each. Place the banana slices on a plate and place in freezer for 2 hours. Enjoy your frozen banana snack on a hot summer day!

Yogurt Parfaits

Prep Time: 15 minutes

Cook Time: 0 minutes

Yield: 4 servings, Good for all ages!

Ingredients: 2 cups fresh fruit, at least 2 different kinds (can also be thawed fresh fruit)
1 cup low-fat plain or soy yogurt
4 TBSP 100% fruit spread
1 cup granola or dry cereal

Directions: Wash and cut fruit into small pieces. In a bowl, mix the yogurt and fruit spread together. Layer each of the four parfaits as follows: Fruit Yogurt Granola (repeat) Enjoy!

Frozen Grapes

Prep Time: 10 minutes

Freezer Time: 2 hours

Yield: 4 servings, Good for all ages!

Ingredients: Seedless grapes

Directions: Wash seedless grapes and separate them from their stem. Place into a bowl or plastic bag. Put them into the freezer for 2 hours. Enjoy your cold, sweet and crunchy treat!

Fruit Smoothies

Prep Time: 5 minutes

Cook Time: 0 minutes

Yield: 2 servings, Good for all ages!

Ingredients: 1 cup berries, fresh or frozen
4 ounces Greek yogurt
1/2 cup 100% apple juice
1 banana, cut into chunks
4 ice cubes

Directions: Place apple juice, yogurt, berries and banana into blender. Cover and blend until smooth. While the blender is running, drop ice cubes into the blender one at a time. Blend until smooth. Pour and enjoy!

2-3 • © Summer Fit Activities™